# Fundamentals of Item Response Theory

# MEASUREMENT METHODS FOR THE SOCIAL SCIENCES SERIES

**Measurement Methods for the Social Sciences** is a series designed to provide professionals and students in the social sciences and education with succinct and illuminating texts on measurement methodology. Beginning with the foundations of measurement theory and encompassing applications on the cutting edge of social science measurement, each volume is expository, limited in its mathematical demands, and designed for self-study as well as formal instruction. Volumes are richly illustrated; each includes exercises with solutions enabling readers to validate their understanding and confirm their learning.

Titles in this series . . .

1. GENERALIZABILITY THEORY: A PRIMER
   Richard J. Shavelson and Noreen M. Webb
2. FUNDAMENTALS OF ITEM RESPONSE THEORY
   Ronald K. Hambleton, H. Swaminathan, and H. Jane Rogers

# Fundamentals of Item Response Theory

## Ronald K. Hambleton
## H. Swaminathan
## H. Jane Rogers

**SAGE** PUBLICATIONS
*The International Professional Publishers*
Newbury Park   London   New Delhi

*For information address:*

SAGE Publications, Inc.
2455 Teller Road
Newbury Park, California 91320

SAGE Publications Ltd.
6 Bonhill Street
London EC2A 4PU
United Kingdom

SAGE Publications India Pvt. Ltd.
M-32 Market
Greater Kailash I
New Delhi 110 048 India

Printed in the United States of America

Library of Congress Cataloging-in-Publication Data


Hambleton, Ronald K.
    Fundamentals of item response theory / Ronald K. Hambleton, H. Swaminathan, H. Jane Rogers.
        p.   cm. — (Measurement methods for the social sciences ; v. 2)
    Includes bibliographical references and index.
    ISBN 0-8039-3646-X (cloth). — ISBN 0-8039-3647-8 (pbk.)
    1. Item response theory.   I. Swaminathan, Hariharan.   II. Rogers, H. Jane.   III. Title.   IV. Series.
BF176.H34   1991                                              91-22005
150′.28′7—dc20


92  93  94  15  14  13  12  11  10  9  8  7  6  5  4  3  2

Sage Production Editor: Diane S. Foster

# Contents

# Series Editor's Foreword

In the last decade we have witnessed a revolution in educational and psychological measurement as the application of classical measurement theory has given way to the use of item response theory (IRT). Today, IRT is used commonly by the largest testing companies in the United States and Europe for design of tests, test assembly, test scaling and calibration, construction of test item banks, investigations of test item bias, and other common procedures in the test development process. Measurement researchers, public school systems, the military, and several civilian branches of the federal government as well, have endorsed and employed IRT with increasing enthusiasm and frequency.

This book provides a lucid but rigorous introduction to the fundamental concepts of item response theory, followed by thorough, accessible descriptions of the application of IRT methods to problems in test construction, identification of potentially biased test items, test equating, and computerized-adaptive testing. A summary of new directions in IRT research and development completes the book.

Hambleton, Swaminathan and Rogers have developed IRT theory and application through carefully wrought arguments, appeals to familiar concepts from classical measurement methods and basic statistics, and extensively described, step-by-step numerical examples. The book is well illustrated with tables containing the results of actual IRT analyses and figures that portray the influence on IRT results of such fundamental issues as models with differing numbers of item parameters, examinees at differing levels of ability, and varying degrees of congruence ("fit") between sets of data and IRT models.

Although equations necessary to compute most IRT statistics are provided in the book, their mathematical derivations have been omitted. Nevertheless, this is not a "cookbook" on IRT methods. The reader will find thorough discussion of alternative procedures for estimating IRT parameters—maximum likelihood estimation, marginal maximum likelihood estimation, Bayesian estimation, and so on. Knowledge of the underlying calculus is *not* required to understand the origins of these procedures and the distinctions among them. Hambleton et al. have been faithful to the goal of the **Measurement Methods for the Social Sciences** series, to make complex measurement concepts, topics, and methods accessible to readers with limited mathematical backgrounds but a keen desire to understand, as well as use, methods that are on the cutting edge of social science assessment. This book introduces powerful new measurement concepts and applications in ways that can be understood and used correctly by thousands for whom IRT heretofore has been no more than a fascinating mystery.

RICHARD M. JAEGER
University of North Carolina at Greensboro

# Preface

The popular (or classical) measurement models and procedures for constructing educational and psychological tests and interpreting test scores have served testing specialists well for a long time. A review of test catalogs and recent editions of the *Mental Measurements Yearbook* and *Test Critiques* would reveal that numerous achievement, aptitude, and personality tests have been constructed using these classical models and procedures. The ways in which educational and psychological tests usually are constructed, evaluated, and used have many well-documented shortcomings of, however (see, for example, Hambleton, 1989). These shortcomings include (a) use of item indices whose values depend on the particular group of examinees with which they are obtained, and (b) examinee ability estimates that depend on the particular choice of items selected for a test.

Psychometricians have advanced a new measurement system, *item response theory* (IRT), to address these and other shortcomings of common measurement practices. In the 1980s, item response theory was one of the dominant topics of study among measurement specialists. Many IRT models of current interest will be described in this book. Because item response theory provides a useful framework for solving a wide variety of measurement problems, many test publishers, state and provincial departments of education, credentialing agencies, school districts, armed forces, and industries use item response theory to assist in building tests, identifying potentially biased test items, equating scores from different tests or different forms of the same test, and reporting test scores. Item response theory has many other promising applications as well. Several of these applications will be discussed in some detail in this book.

Why publish an IRT book at this time? Interest in learning about this new measurement theory and in applying it is worldwide, and the need exists for practical instructional material. The purpose of this book, therefore, is to provide a comprehensive and practical introduction to the field of item response theory. The limitations of classical measurement procedures are addressed to provide a rationale for an alternative psychometric model. The fundamentals of item response theory, including models, assumptions, and properties, as well as parameter estimation, procedures for assessing model-data fit, alternative reporting scales, and item and test information and efficiency constitute the central part of the book. Several important IRT applications are described in later chapters. Connections between classical test theory and item response theory are made wherever possible to enhance the clarity of the material.

Since the book is intended for newcomers to the IRT field with modest statistical skills, our approach focuses on the conceptual basis of item response theory and avoids discussion of mathematical derivations or complex statistical aspects of the theory. Follow-up references are given for these important aspects. Examples and illustrations are used as often as possible. Exercises and complete answers are included at the end of each chapter to enable practitioners to gain experience with IRT models and procedures. Finally, some of the popular IRT computer programs are introduced, along with a discussion of their strengths and weaknesses. Information about the computer programs should facilitate the successful application of IRT models.

In summary, IRT consists of a family of models that have been demonstrated to be useful in the design, construction, and evaluation of educational and psychological tests. As further research is carried out, the remaining technical problems associated with applying the models should be resolved. In addition, it is expected that newer and more applicable IRT models will be developed in the coming years, enabling IRT to provide even better solutions to important measurement problems. We hope that this book will be useful to measurement specialists who wish to explore the utility of IRT in their own work.

We are grateful to several colleagues, former students, and current students who provided extensive reviews of an earlier draft of this book: Lloyd Bond, University of North Carolina at Greensboro; Linda L. Cook and Daniel Eignor, Educational Testing Service; Wendy Yen and Anne Fitzpatrick, CTB/Macmillan/McGraw-Hill; and Russell W. Jones, University of Massachusetts at Amherst. Their comments often forced us to clarify our discussions and positions on various technical matters. The book is more readable and technically correct because of our reviewers' insights and experience.

# 1

# Background

Consider a typical measurement practitioner. Dr. Testmaker works for a company that specializes in the development and analysis of achievement and aptitude tests. The tests developed by Dr. Testmaker's company are used in awarding high school diplomas, promoting students from one grade to the next, evaluating the quality of education, identifying workers in need of training, and credentialing practitioners in a wide variety of professions. Dr. Testmaker knows that the company's clients expect high quality tests, tests that meet their needs and that can stand up technically to legal challenges. Dr. Testmaker refers to the AERA/APA/NCME *Standards for Educational and Psychological Testing* (1985) and is familiar with the details of a number of lawsuits that have arisen because of questions about test quality or test misuse.

Dr. Testmaker's company uses classical test theory models and methods to address most of its technical problems (e.g., item selection, reliability assessment, test score equating), but recently its clients have been suggesting—and sometimes requiring—that *item response theory* (IRT) be used with their tests. Dr. Testmaker has only a rudimentary knowledge of item response theory and no previous experience in applying it, and consequently he has many questions, such as the following:

1. What IRT models are available, and which model should be used?
2. Which of the many available algorithms should be used to estimate parameters?
3. Which IRT computer program should be used to analyze the data?
4. How can the fit of the chosen IRT model to the test data be determined?
5. What is the relationship between test length and the precision of ability estimates?

6. How can IRT item statistics be used to construct tests to meet content and technical specifications?
7. How can IRT be used to evaluate the statistical consequences of changing items in a test?
8. How can IRT be used to assess the relative utility of different tests that are measuring the same ability?
9. How can IRT be used to detect the presence of potentially biased test items?
10. How can IRT be used to place test item statistics obtained from nonequivalent samples of examinees on a common scale?

The purpose of this book is to provide an introduction to item response theory that will address the above questions and many others. Specifically, it will (a) introduce the basic concepts and most popular models of item response theory, (b) address parameter estimation and available computer programs, (c) demonstrate approaches to assessing model-data fit, (d) describe the scales on which abilities and item characteristics are reported, and (e) describe the application of IRT to test construction, detection of differential item functioning, equating, and adaptive testing. The book is intended to be oriented practically, and numerous examples are presented to highlight selected technical points.

## Limitations of Classical Measurement Models

Dr. Testmaker's clients are turning towards item response theory because classical testing methods and measurement procedures have a number of shortcomings. Perhaps the most important shortcoming is that examinee characteristics and test characteristics cannot be separated: each can be interpreted only in the context of the other. The examinee characteristic we are interested in is the "ability" measured by the test. What do we mean by ability? In the classical test theory framework, the notion of ability is expressed by the *true score,* which is defined as "the expected value of observed performance *on the test of interest.*" An examinee's ability is defined only in terms of a particular test. When the test is "hard," the examinee will appear to have low ability; when the test is "easy," the examinee will appear to have higher ability. What do we mean by "hard" and "easy" tests? The *difficulty of a test item* is defined as "the proportion of examines *in a group of interest* who answer the item correctly." Whether an item is hard or easy depends on the ability of the examinees being measured, and the ability of the examinees depends on whether the test items are hard or easy! Item discrimination and test score reliability and validity are also defined in terms of a particular group of examinees. Test and item characteristics change as the examinee context changes, and examinee characteristics change as the test context changes. Hence, it is very difficult to compare examinees who take different tests and very difficult to compare items whose characteristics are obtained using different groups of examinees. (This is not to say that such comparisons are impossible: Measurement specialists have devised procedures to deal with these problems in practice, but the conceptual problem remains.)

Let us look at the practical consequences of item characteristics that depend on the group of examinees from which they are obtained, that is, are *group-dependent*. Group-dependent item indices are of limited use when constructing tests for examinee populations that are dissimilar to the population of examinees with which the item indices were obtained. This limitation can be a major one for test developers, who often have great difficulty securing examinees for field tests of new instruments—especially examinees who can represent the population for whom the test is intended. Consider, for example, the problem of field-testing items for a state proficiency test administered in the spring of each year. Examinees included in a field test in the fall will, necessarily, be less capable than those examinees tested in the spring. Hence, items will appear more difficult in the field test than they will appear in the spring test administration. A variation on the same problem arises with item banks, which are becoming widely used in test construction. Suppose the goal is to expand the bank by adding a new set of test items along with their item indices. If these new item indices are obtained on a group of examinees different from the groups who took the items already in the bank, the comparability of item indices must be questioned.

What are the consequences of examinee scores that depend on the particular set of items administered, that is, are *test-dependent?* Clearly, it is difficult to compare examinees who take different tests: The scores on the two tests are on different scales, and no functional relationship exists between the scales. Even if the examinees are given the same or parallel tests, a problem remains. When the examinees are of different ability (i.e., the test is more difficult for one group than for the other), their test scores contain different amounts of error. To demonstrate this point intuitively, consider an examinee who obtains a score of zero: This score tells us that the examinee's ability is low but provides no information about exactly how low. On the other hand, when an examinee gets some items right and some wrong, the test score contains information about what the examinee can and cannot do, and thus gives a more precise measure of ability. If the test scores for two examinees are not equally precise measures of ability, how may comparisons between the test scores be made? To obtain scores for two examinees that contain equal amounts of error (i.e., scores that are equally reliable), we can match test difficulty with the approximate ability levels of the examinees; yet, when several forms of a test that differ substantially in difficulty are used, test scores are, again, not comparable. Consider two examinees who perform at the 50% level on two tests that differ substantially in difficulty: These examinees cannot be considered equivalent in ability. How different are they? How may two examinees be compared when they receive different scores on tests that differ in difficulty but measure the same ability? These problems are difficult to resolve within the framework of classical measurement theory.

Two more sources of dissatisfaction with classical test theory lie in the definition of reliability and what may be thought of as its conceptual converse, the standard error of measurement. *Reliability,* in a classical test theory framework, is defined as "the correlation between test scores on parallel forms of a test." In practice, satisfying the definition of *parallel tests* is difficult, if not impossible. The various reliability coefficients available provide either lower bound estimates of reliability or reliability estimates with unknown biases (Hambleton & van der Linden, 1982). The problem with the standard error of measurement, which is a function of test score reliability and variance, is that it is assumed to be the same for all examinees. But as pointed out above, scores on any test are unequally precise measures for examinees of different ability. Hence, the assumption of equal errors of measurement for all examinees is implausible (Lord, 1984).

A final limitation of classical test theory is that it is test oriented rather than item oriented. The classical true score model provides no consideration of how examinees respond to a given item. Hence, no basis exists for determining how well a particular examinee might do when confronted with a test item. More specifically, classical test theory does not enable us to make predictions about how an individual or a group of examinees will perform on a given item. Such questions as, What is the probability of an examinee answering a given item correctly? are important in a number of testing applications. Such information is necessary, for example, if a test designer wants to predict test score characteristics for one or more populations of examinees or to design tests with particular characteristics for certain populations of examinees. For example, a test intended to discriminate well among scholarship candidates may be desired.

In addition to the limitations mentioned above, classical measurement models and procedures have provided less-than-ideal solutions to many testing problems—for example, the design of tests (Lord, 1980), the identification of biased items (Lord, 1980), adaptive testing (Weiss, 1983), and the equating of test scores (Cook & Eignor, 1983, 1989).

For these reasons, psychometricians have sought alternative theories and models of mental measurement. The desirable features of an alternative test theory would include (a) item characteristics that are *not* group-dependent, (b) scores describing examinee proficiency that are *not* test-dependent, (c) a model that is expressed at the item level rather than at the test level, (d) a model that does *not* require strictly parallel tests for assessing reliability, and (e) a model that provides a measure of precision for each ability score. It has been shown that these features can be obtained within the framework of an alternative test theory known as *item response theory* (Hambleton, 1983; Hambleton & Swaminathan, 1985; Lord, 1980; Wright & Stone, 1979).

## Exercises for Chapter 1

1. Identify four of the limitations of classical test theory that have stimulated measurement specialists to pursue alternative measurement models.

2. Item responses on a test item and total test scores for 30 examinees are given in Table 1.1. The first 15 examinees were classified as "low ability" based on their total scores; the second 15 examinees were classified as "high ability."

   a. Calculate the proportion of examinees in each group who answered the item correctly (this is the classical item difficulty index in each group).

   b. Compute the item-total correlation in each group (this is the classical item discrimination index in each group).

   c. What can you conclude regarding the invariance of the classical item indices?

**TABLE 1.1**

| | Low-Ability Group | | | High-Ability Group | |
|---|---|---|---|---|---|
| Examinee | Item Response | Total Score | Examinee | Item Response | Total Score |
| 1 | 0 | 8 | 16 | 1 | 33 |
| 2 | 0 | 12 | 17 | 0 | 28 |
| 3 | 0 | 6 | 18 | 1 | 29 |
| 4 | 0 | 12 | 19 | 1 | 30 |
| 5 | 0 | 8 | 20 | 1 | 29 |
| 6 | 0 | 8 | 21 | 0 | 28 |
| 7 | 0 | 8 | 22 | 1 | 33 |
| 8 | 0 | 11 | 23 | 1 | 32 |
| 9 | 1 | 13 | 24 | 1 | 32 |
| 10 | 0 | 4 | 25 | 1 | 33 |
| 11 | 1 | 14 | 26 | 0 | 34 |
| 12 | 1 | 13 | 27 | 1 | 35 |
| 13 | 0 | 10 | 28 | 1 | 34 |
| 14 | 0 | 9 | 29 | 1 | 38 |
| 15 | 0 | 8 | 30 | 1 | 37 |

## Answers to Exercises for Chapter 1

1. Item-dependent ability scores, sample-dependent item statistics, no probability information available about how examinees of specific abilities might perform on certain test items, restriction of equal measurement errors for all examinees.

2. a. Low-scoring group: $p = 0.2$. High-scoring group: $p = 0.8$.

   b. Low-scoring group: $r = 0.68$. High-scoring group: $r = 0.39$.

   c. Classical item indices are not invariant across subpopulations.

# 2

## Concepts, Models, and Features

### Basic Ideas

Item response theory (IRT) rests on two basic postulates: (a) The performance of an examinee on a test item can be predicted (or explained) by a set of factors called traits, latent traits, or abilities; and (b) the relationship between examinees' item performance and the set of traits underlying item performance can be described by a monotonically increasing function called an *item characteristic function* or *item characteristic curve* (ICC). This function specifies that as the level of the trait increases, the probability of a correct response to an item increases. Figure 2.1 shows an item characteristic function for the case when only one trait underlies performance on the item, together with distributions of ability for two groups of examinees. Observe that examinees with higher values on the trait have higher probabilities of answering the item correctly than do examinees with lower values on the trait, regardless of group membership.

Many possible item response models exist, differing in the mathematical form of the item characteristic function and/or the number of parameters specified in the model. All IRT models contain one or more parameters describing the item and one or more parameters describing the examinee. The first step in any IRT application is to estimate these parameters. Procedures for parameter estimation are discussed in chapter 3.

Item response models, unlike the classical true score model, are *falsifiable* models. A given item response model may or may not be appropriate for a particular set of test data; that is, the model may not adequately predict or explain the data. In any IRT application, it is essential to assess the fit of the model to the data. Procedures for assessing model-data fit are discussed in chapter 4.

7

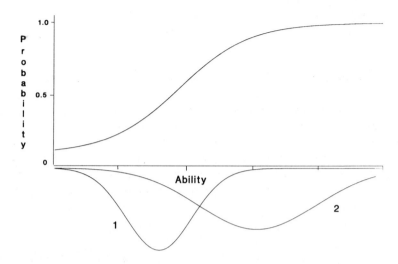

**Figure 2.1.** An Item Characteristic Curve and Distributions of Ability for Two Groups of Examinees

When a given IRT model fits the test data of interest, several desirable features are obtained. Examinee ability estimates are not test-dependent, and item indices are not group-dependent. Ability estimates obtained from different sets of items will be the same (except for measurement errors), and item parameter estimates obtained in different groups of examinees will be the same (except for measurement errors). In item response theory, item and ability parameters are said to be *invariant*. The property of invariance of item and ability parameters is obtained by incorporating information about the items into the ability-estimation process and by incorporating information about the examinees' abilities into the item-parameter-estimation process. The invariance of item parameters is illustrated in Figure 2.1, which shows distributions of ability for two groups of examinees. Note that examinees of the same ability have the same probability of giving a correct response to the item, regardless of whether they are from Group 1 or Group 2. Since the probability of success for an examinee with given ability is determined by the item's parameters, the item parameters must also be the same for the two groups.

In addition to the desirable features mentioned above, IRT provides estimates of standard errors for individual ability estimates, rather than a single estimate of error for all examinees, as is the case in classical test theory.

## Assumptions

The mathematical models employed in IRT specify that an examinee's probability of answering a given item correctly depends on the examinee's ability or abilities and the characteristics of the item. IRT models include a set of assumptions about the data to which the model is applied. Although the viability of assumptions cannot be determined directly, some indirect evidence can be collected and assessed, and the overall fit of the model to the test data can be assessed as well (see chapter 4).

An assumption common to the IRT models most widely used is that only one ability is measured by the items that make up the test. This is called the assumption of *unidimensionality*. A concept related to unidimensionality is that of *local independence*. Unidimensionality and local independence are discussed in the next section.

Another assumption made in all IRT models is that the item characteristic function specified reflects the true relationship among the unobservable variables (abilities) and observable variables (item responses). Assumptions are made also about the item characteristics that are relevant to an examinee's performance on an item. The major distinction among the IRT models in common use is in the number and type of item characteristics assumed to affect examinee performance. These assumptions will be discussed shortly.

### Unidimensionality

As stated above, a common assumption of IRT models is that only one ability is measured by a set of items in a test. This assumption cannot be strictly met because several cognitive, personality, and test-taking factors always affect test performance, at least to some extent. These factors might include level of motivation, test anxiety, ability to work quickly, tendency to guess when in doubt about answers, and cognitive skills in addition to the dominant one measured by the set of test items. What is required for the unidimensionality assumption to be met adequately by a set of test data is the presence of a "dominant" component or factor that influences test performance. This dominant component or factor is referred to as the ability measured by the test; it should be noted, however, that ability is not necessarily inherent or unchangeable. Ability scores may be expected to change over time because of learning, forgetting, and other factors.

Item response models in which a single dominant ability is presumed sufficient to explain or account for examinee performance are referred to as *unidimensional* models. Models in which it is assumed that more than one ability is necessary to account for examinee test performance are referred to as *multidimensional*. These latter models are more complex and, to date, have not been well developed (McDonald, 1981).

### Local Independence

Local independence means that when the abilities influencing test performance are held constant, examinees' responses to any pair of items are statistically independent. In other words, after taking examinees' abilities into account, no relationship exists between examinees' responses to different items. Simply put, this means that the abilities specified in the model are the only factors influencing examinees' responses to test items. This set of abilities represents the *complete latent space*. When the assumption of unidimensionality holds, the complete latent space consists of only one ability.

To state the definition of local independence more formally, let $\theta$ be the complete set of abilities assumed to influence the performance of an examinee on the test. Let $U_i$ be the response of a randomly chosen examinee to item $i$ ($i = 1, 2, \ldots, n$). Let $P(U_i \mid \theta)$ denote the probability of the response of a randomly chosen examinee with ability $\theta$; $P(U_i = 1 \mid \theta)$[1] denotes the probability of a correct response, and $P(U_i = 0 \mid \theta)$ denotes the probability of an incorrect response. The property of local independence can be stated mathematically in the following way:

$$\text{Prob}(U_1, U_2, \ldots, U_n \mid \theta) = P(U_1 \mid \theta)\, P(U_2 \mid \theta) \ldots P(U_n \mid \theta)$$

$$= \prod_{i=1}^{n} P(U_i \mid \theta)$$

The property of local independence means that for a given examinee (or all examinees at a given ability value) the probability of a response pattern on a set of items is equal to the product of probabilities associated with the examinee's responses to the individual items. For example, if the response pattern for an examinee on three items is (1, 1, 0), that is, $U_1 = 1$, $U_2 = 1$, and $U_3 = 0$, then the assumption of local of independence implies that

$$P(U_1 = 1, U_2 = 1, U_3 = 0 \mid \theta) = P(U_1 = 1 \mid \theta) P(U_2 = 1 \mid \theta) P(U_3 = 0 \mid \theta)$$

$$= P_1 P_2 Q_3$$

where

$$P_i = P(U_i = 1 \mid \theta) \quad \text{and} \quad Q_i = 1 - P_i$$

The notion of local independence described above may seem counterintuitive. An examinee's responses to several test items cannot be expected to be uncorrelated; that is, the responses are unlikely to be independent. In what sense, then, can local independence hold? When variables are correlated, they have some traits in common. When these traits are "partialled out" or "held constant," the variables become uncorrelated. This is the basic principle underlying factor analysis. Similarly, in item response theory, the relationships among an examinee's responses to several test items are due to the traits (abilities) influencing performance on the items. After "partialling out" the abilities (i.e., conditioning on ability), the examinee's responses to the items are likely to be independent. For this reason, the assumption of local independence can also be referred to as the assumption of conditional independence.

When the assumption of unidimensionality is true, local independence is obtained: in this sense, the two concepts are equivalent (Lord, 1980; Lord & Novick, 1968). Local independence can be obtained, however, *even when the data set is not unidimensional.* Local independence will be obtained whenever the complete latent space has been specified; that is, when all the ability dimensions influencing performance have been taken into account.

Conversely, local independence does not hold when the complete latent space has not been specified. For example, on a mathematics test item that requires a high level of reading skill, examinees with poor reading skills will not answer the item correctly regardless of their mathematical proficiency. Hence, a dimension other than mathematical proficiency will influence performance on the item; if a unidimensional IRT model is fitted to the data, local independence will not hold. On the other hand, if all the examinees have the requisite reading skills, only mathematical proficiency will influence performance on the item and local independence will be obtained when a unidimensional model is fitted. Local independence also may not hold when a test item contains a clue to the correct answer, or provides information that is helpful in answering another item. In this case, some examinees will detect the clue and some examinees will not. The ability to detect the clue is a dimension other than the ability being tested. If a unidimensional model is fitted, local independence will not hold.

## Popular Models in Item Response Theory

An item characteristic function or item characteristic curve (ICC) is a mathematical expression that relates the probability of success (i.e., giving a correct response) on an item to the ability measured by the test and the characteristics of the item. While it is possible to conceive of an infinite number of IRT models, only a few models are in current use. A primary distinction among the most popular unidimensional item response models is in the number of parameters used to describe items. The choice of model is up to the user, but this choice involves assumptions about the data that can be verified later by examining how well the model "explains" the observed test results. The three most popular unidimensional IRT models are the one-, two-, and three-parameter logistic models, so named because of the number of item parameters each incorporates. These models are appropriate for dichotomous item response data.

### One-Parameter Logistic Model

The one-parameter logistic model is one of the most widely used IRT models. Item characteristic curves for the one-parameter logistic model are given by the equation

$$P_i(\theta) = \frac{e^{(\theta - b_i)}}{1 + e^{(\theta - b_i)}} \qquad i = 1, 2, \ldots, n \qquad [2.1]$$

where

$P_i(\theta)$    is the probability that a randomly chosen examinee with ability $\theta$ answers item $i$ correctly,

$b_i$    is the item $i$ difficulty parameter,

$n$    is the number of items in the test,

$e$    is a transcendental number (like $\pi$) whose value is 2.718 (correct to three decimals), and

$P_i(\theta)$    is an S-shaped curve with values between 0 and 1 over the ability scale.

The $b_i$ parameter for an item is the point on the ability scale where the probability of a correct response is 0.5. This parameter is a location parameter, indicating the position of the ICC in relation to the ability scale. The greater the value of the $b_i$ parameter, the greater the ability that is required for an examinee to have a 50% chance of getting the item right; hence, the harder the item. Difficult items are located to the right or the higher end of the ability scale; easy items are located to the left or the lower end of the ability scale.

When the ability values of a group are transformed so that their mean is 0 and their standard deviation is 1, the values of $b_i$ vary (typically) from about −2.0 to +2.0. Values of $b_i$ near −2.0 correspond to items that are very easy, and values of $b_i$ near 2.0 correspond to items that are very difficult for the group of examinees.

Some sample ICCs for the one-parameter model are shown in Figure 2.2. The item parameters are as follows: for Item 1, $b_1 = 1.0$; for Item 2, $b_2 = 2.0$; for Item 3, $b_3 = -1.0$; and for Item 4, $b_4 = 0.0$. Note that the curves differ only by their location on the ability scale. In the one-parameter model, it is assumed that item difficulty is the only item characteristic that influences examinee performance. No item parameter corresponds to the classical test theory item discrimination index; in effect, this is equivalent to the assumption that all items are equally discriminating. Note also that the lower asymptote of the ICC is zero: this specifies that examinees of very low ability have zero probability of correctly answering the item. Thus, no allowance is made for the possibility that low-ability examinees may guess, as they are likely to do on multiple-choice items.

Clearly, the one-parameter model is based on restrictive assumptions. The appropriateness of these assumptions depends on the nature of the data and the importance of the intended application. For example, the assumptions may be quite acceptable for relatively easy tests

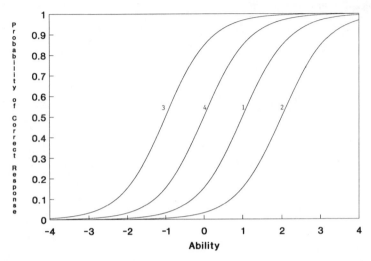

**Figure 2.2.** One-Parameter Item Characteristic Curves for Four Typical Items

constructed from a homogeneous bank of test items. Such situations may arise with some criterion-referenced tests following effective instruction.

The one-parameter logistic model is often called the Rasch model, in honor of its developer. While the form of Rasch's model is different from that presented here, the one-parameter logistic model is mathematically equivalent to Rasch's model. For details of the development of the Rasch model, refer to Rasch (1960) and Wright and Stone (1979).

*Two-Parameter Logistic Model*

Lord (1952) was the first to develop a two-parameter item response model, based on the cumulative normal distribution (normal ogive). Birnbaum (1968) substituted the two-parameter logistic function for the two-parameter normal ogive function as the form of the item characteristic function. Logistic functions have the important advantage of being more convenient to work with than normal ogive functions. The logistic model is more mathematically tractable than the normal ogive model because the latter involves integration, whereas the former is an explicit function of item and ability parameters and also has important statistical properties.

Item characteristic curves for the two-parameter logistic model developed by Birnbaum are given by the equation

$$P_i(\theta) = \frac{e^{Da_i(\theta - b_i)}}{1 + e^{Da_i(\theta - b_i)}} \qquad i = 1, 2, \ldots, n \qquad [2.2]$$

where the parameters $P_i(\theta)$ and $b_i$ are defined just as in Equation 2.1. As is easily seen, the two-parameter logistic model resembles the one-parameter model except for the presence of two additional elements. The factor $D$ is a scaling factor introduced to make the logistic function as close as possible to the normal ogive function. It has been shown that when $D = 1.7$, values of $P_i(\theta)$ for the two-parameter normal ogive and the two-parameter logistic models differ in absolute value by less than 0.01 for all values of $\theta$.

The second additional element of the two-parameter model is the parameter $a_i$, which is called the item discrimination parameter. The $a_i$ parameter is proportional to the slope of the ICC at the point $b_i$ on the ability scale. Items with steeper slopes are more useful for separating examinees into different ability levels than are items with less steep slopes. In fact, the usefulness of an item for discriminating among examinees near an ability level $\theta$ (separating examinees with abilities $\leq \theta$ from examinees with abilities $> \theta$) is proportional to the slope of the ICC at $\theta$.

The item discrimination parameter is defined, theoretically, on the scale $(-\infty, +\infty)$. Negatively discriminating items are discarded from ability tests, however, because something is wrong with an item (such as miskeying) if the probability of answering it correctly decreases as examinee ability increases. Also, it is unusual to obtain $a_i$ values larger than 2. Hence, the usual range for item discrimination parameters is $(0, 2)$. High values of $a_i$ result in item characteristic functions that are very "steep," and low values of $a_i$ lead to item characteristic functions that increase gradually as a function of ability. Readers interested in experimenting by changing values of item parameters to determine their effects on ICCs are referred to some computer software for the IBM PC and the APPLE computers by Baker (1985), and to an introductory article on logistic models by Harris (1989).

The two-parameter model is obviously a generalization of the one-parameter model that allows for differently discriminating items. Some sample ICCs for the two-parameter model are shown in Figure 2.3. For

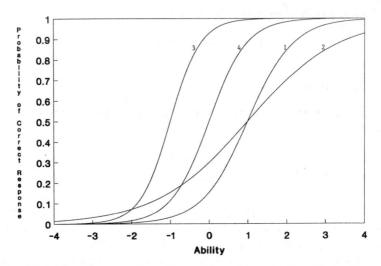

**Figure 2.3.** Two-Parameter Item Characteristic Curves for Four Typical Items

Item 1, $b_1 = 1.0$ and $a_1 = 1.0$; for Item 2, $b_2 = 1.0$ and $a_2 = 0.5$; for Item 3, $b_3 = -1.0$ and $a_3 = 1.5$; for Item 4, $b_4 = 0.0$ and $a_4 = 1.2$. The ICCs are not parallel, as they were for the one-parameter model. Each ICC has a different slope, reflecting the fact that the discrimination parameter values are different. Note again that the lower asymptote of each curve is zero; hence, the two-parameter model, like the one-parameter model, makes no allowance for guessing behavior. The assumption of no guessing is most plausible with free-response items, but it often can be met approximately with multiple-choice items when a test is not too difficult for the examinees. For example, this assumption may be met when competency tests are administered to students following effective instruction.

An alternative and somewhat more convenient way to write $P_i(\theta)$ for the two-parameter logistic model (and the three-parameter model, too) is this: If the numerator and denominator of Equation 2.2 are divided by $e^{Da_i(\theta - b_i)}$, then $P_i(\theta)$ becomes

$$P_i(\theta) = \frac{1}{1 + e^{-Da_i(\theta - b_i)}}$$

which can be written more compactly as

$$P_i(\theta) = [1 + e^{-Da_i(\theta - b_i)}]^{-1}.$$

## Three-Parameter Logistic Model

The mathematical expression for the three-parameter logistic model is

$$P_i(\theta) = c_i + (1 - c_i) \frac{e^{Da_i(\theta - b_i)}}{1 + e^{Da_i(\theta - b_i)}} \qquad i = 1, 2, \ldots, n \quad [2.3]$$

where $P_i(\theta)$, $b_i$, $a_i$, and $D$ are defined as for the two-parameter model. The additional parameter in the model, $c_i$, is called the *pseudo-chance-level* parameter. This parameter provides a (possibly) nonzero lower asymptote for the item characteristic curve and represents the probability of examinees with low ability answering the item correctly.

The parameter $c_i$ is incorporated into the model to take into account performance at the low end of the ability continuum, where guessing is a factor in test performance on selected-response (e.g., multiple choice) test items. Typically, $c_i$ assumes values that are smaller than the value that would result if examinees guessed randomly on the item. As Lord (1974) has noted, this phenomenon probably can be attributed to the ingenuity of item workers in developing attractive but incorrect choices. For this reason, $c_i$ should not be called the "guessing parameter."

Six typical three-parameter logistic ICCs are displayed in Figure 2.4. The corresponding item parameters are displayed in Table 2.1. The comparison of Items 1 to 3 with Items 4 to 6 (but especially the comparison of Items 1 and 4) highlights the role of the item difficulty parameter in the location of ICCs. More difficult items (Items 1, 2, 3) are shifted to the higher end of the ability scale, while easier items are shifted to the lower end of the ability scale. The comparison of Items 1 and 2 (or Items 1, 3, and 4 with Items 2, 5, and 6) highlights the influence of the item discrimination parameter on the steepness of ICCs. Finally, a comparison of Items 1 and 3 highlights the role of the $c$ parameter ($c_i$) in the shape of ICCs. A comparison of the different lower asymptotes of Items 3, 5, and 6 is also informative.

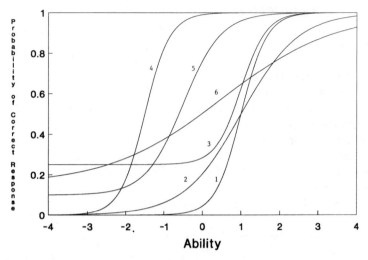

**Figure 2.4.** Three-Parameter Item Characteristic Curves for Six Typical Items

## The Property of Invariance

The property of invariance of item and ability parameters is the cornerstone of IRT and its major distinction from classical test theory. This property implies that the parameters that characterize an item do not depend on the ability distribution of the examinees and the parameter that characterizes an examinee does not depend on the set of test items.

**TABLE 2.1** Item Parameters for Six Typical Test Items

| Test Item | Item Parameter | | |
| | $b_i$ | $a_i$ | $c_i$ |
|---|---|---|---|
| 1 | 1.00 | 1.80 | 0.00 |
| 2 | 1.00 | 0.80 | 0.00 |
| 3 | 1.00 | 1.80 | 0.25 |
| 4 | −1.50 | 1.80 | 0.00 |
| 5 | −0.50 | 1.20 | 0.10 |
| 6 | 0.50 | 0.40 | 0.15 |

As noted earlier, the property of invariance of item parameters can be observed in Figure 2.1. When the IRT model fits the data, the same ICC is obtained for the test item regardless of the distribution of ability in the group of examinees used to estimate the item parameters. Hence, the ICC is invariant across the two populations.

To some researchers, the property of item invariance may seem surprising. The property, however, is a well-known feature of the linear regression model. In the linear regression model, the regression line for predicting a variable $Y$ from a variable $X$ is obtained as the line joining the means of the $Y$ variable for each value of the $X$ variable. When the regression model holds, the same regression line will be obtained within any restricted range of the $X$ variable, that is, in any subpopulation on $X$, meaning that the slope and intercept of the line will be the same in any subpopulation on $X$. A derived index such as the correlation coefficient, which is not a parameter that characterizes the regression line, is *not* invariant across subpopulations. The difference between the slope parameter and the correlation coefficient is that the slope parameter does not depend on the characteristics of the subpopulation, such as its variability, whereas the correlation coefficient does (note, however, that the proper *estimation* of the line does require a heterogeneous sample). The same concepts also apply in item response models, which can be regarded as nonlinear regression models.

To illustrate the property of invariance of item parameters and to understand the conditions under which invariance holds, consider the following example, in which the responses of 90 examinees to a 40-item test were generated to fit a two-parameter logistic item response model (see Equation 2.2). A summary of the responses of the examinees (10 at each of 9 ability levels)—their responses to a particular item on the test and their total scores on the test—is given in Table 2.2. The corresponding plot of probability of success on the selected item against ability, $\theta$, is given in Figure 2.5.

The classical item difficulty, or $p$-value, for the item of interest is 0.5, and the classical item discrimination, or point-biserial correlation between the item score and total score, is 0.65. As a demonstration of the lack of invariance of classical item indices, let us consider the examinees as forming two ability groups: examinees at $\theta$ of $-1.72$, $-1.13$, and $-0.72$ forming the low-ability group and the examinees at $\theta$ of 0.52, 0.92, and 1.52 forming the high-ability group. For the low-ability examinees the $p$-value (based on 30 examinees) is 0.2 and the point-biserial correlation is 0.56. For the high-ability examinees the $p$-value

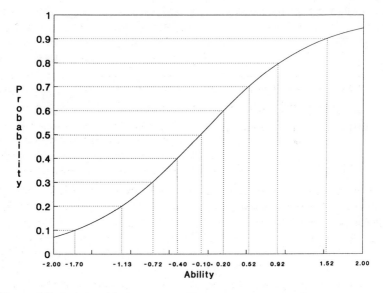

**Figure 2.5.** Relationship Between Ability and Probability of Success on an Item

is 0.8 and the point-biserial correlation is 0.47. These calculations demonstrate that the classical difficulty and discrimination indices change when the examinee ability distribution changes (obviously, restriction of range results in lower point-biserial correlations for each subgroup than for the total group).

Let us now fit separately a two-parameter item response model for the entire group and for the high- and low-ability groups. If invariance holds, the parameters obtained should be identical. Since in the two-parameter model the probability of success for an examinee with ability $\theta$ is given by

$$P = \frac{e^{Da(\theta - b)}}{1 + e^{Da(\theta - b)}}$$

and

$$\frac{P}{1 - P} = e^{Da(\theta - b)}$$

**TABLE 2.2** Ability Level θ, Probability of Success on an Item, Response to the Item, and Total Score for 90 Examinees

| θ | $P(\theta)$ | | Examinee | | | | | | | | | |
|---|---|---|---|---|---|---|---|---|---|---|---|---|
| | | | 1 | 2 | 3 | 4 | 5 | 6 | 7 | 8 | 9 | 10 |
| −1.716 | 0.1 | Item Response: | 0 | 0 | 0 | 0 | 0 | 0 | 0 | 0 | 1 | 0 |
| | | Total Score: | 8 | 12 | 6 | 12 | 8 | 8 | 8 | 11 | 13 | 4 |
| −1.129 | 0.2 | Item Response: | 0 | 1 | 0 | 0 | 0 | 0 | 1 | 0 | 0 | 0 |
| | | Total Score: | 10 | 14 | 9 | 8 | 10 | 11 | 13 | 12 | 7 | 7 |
| −0.723 | 0.3 | Item Response: | 0 | 1 | 0 | 0 | 1 | 1 | 0 | 0 | 0 | 0 |
| | | Total Score: | 11 | 15 | 14 | 13 | 15 | 15 | 13 | 11 | 15 | 13 |
| −0.398 | 0.4 | Item Response: | 0 | 0 | 1 | 0 | 1 | 0 | 1 | 0 | 0 | 1 |
| | | Total Score: | 13 | 12 | 18 | 12 | 17 | 10 | 16 | 15 | 12 | 19 |
| −0.100 | 0.5 | Item Response: | 0 | 1 | 1 | 1 | 1 | 0 | 0 | 0 | 1 | 0 |
| | | Total Score: | 17 | 21 | 25 | 25 | 21 | 19 | 18 | 19 | 20 | 15 |
| 0.198 | 0.6 | Item Response: | 1 | 0 | 1 | 0 | 1 | 0 | 1 | 1 | 1 | 0 |
| | | Total Score: | 21 | 19 | 26 | 22 | 25 | 22 | 24 | 24 | 28 | 19 |
| 0.523 | 0.7 | Item Response: | 1 | 1 | 1 | 0 | 0 | 1 | 1 | 0 | 1 | 1 |
| | | Total Score: | 27 | 26 | 25 | 24 | 24 | 30 | 28 | 24 | 29 | 29 |
| 0.919 | 0.8 | Item Response: | 1 | 0 | 1 | 1 | 1 | 0 | 1 | 1 | 1 | 1 |
| | | Total Score: | 33 | 28 | 29 | 30 | 29 | 28 | 33 | 32 | 32 | 33 |
| 1.516 | 0.9 | Item Response: | 0 | 1 | 1 | 1 | 1 | 1 | 1 | 1 | 1 | 1 |
| | | Total Score: | 34 | 35 | 34 | 38 | 37 | 37 | 36 | 35 | 37 | 39 |

it follows that

$$\ln \frac{P}{1 - P} = Da(\theta - b)$$

$$= \alpha\theta + \beta$$

where $\alpha = Da$ and $\beta = -Dab$. The above relationship is a linear function of $\theta$ with two unknowns, $\alpha$ and $\beta$ (the slope and intercept of the line, respectively), and, hence, their values can be determined exactly if

$P$ and $\theta$ are known at two points. (In reality, determination of item parameters cannot be carried out in this way since $\theta$ will never be known; this procedure is used here for pedagogical purposes only.)

To determine the item parameters based on the *entire range of ability,* we can choose (arbitrarily) $\theta = -1.716$ and $\theta = 1.516$ with corresponding $P$ values of 0.1 and 0.9. Thus, the two equations to be solved are

$$\ln \frac{0.1}{0.9} = \alpha(-1.716) + \beta \qquad \text{and} \qquad \ln \frac{0.9}{0.1} = \alpha(1.516) + \beta$$

Subtracting the first equation from the second, we have

$$\ln \frac{0.9}{0.1} - \ln \frac{0.1}{0.9} = \alpha(1.516) - \alpha(-1.716)$$

Solving for $\alpha$, we obtain

$$\alpha = 1.360.$$

Substituting this value in the second equation gives

$$\beta = 0.136.$$

The values of $a$ and $b$ now can be determined: $a = 0.8$ and $b = -0.1$.

In the low-ability subgroup, $\alpha$ and $\beta$ can be determined using the two points $\theta = -1.716$ and $\theta = -0.723$ with the corresponding $P$ values of 0.1 and 0.3. The equations to be solved are

$$\ln \frac{0.1}{0.9} = \alpha(-1.716) + \beta \qquad \text{and} \qquad \ln \frac{0.3}{0.7} = \alpha(-0.723) + \beta$$

Solving these equations in the same manner as previously, we obtain $\alpha = 1.359$ and $\beta = 0.136$, which in turn yield $a = 0.8$ and $b = -0.1$.

In the high-ability group, we determine $\alpha$ and $\beta$ using the points $\theta = 0.523$ and $\theta = 1.516$ with corresponding $P$ values of 0.7 and 0.9. The equations to be solved in this case are

$$\ln \frac{0.7}{0.3} = \alpha(0.523) + \beta \qquad \text{and} \qquad \ln \frac{0.9}{0.1} = \alpha(1.516) + \beta$$

Solving these equations, we obtain $\alpha = 1.359$ and $\beta = 0.136$, which yield the same $a$ and $b$ values as before. What we have demonstrated is the simple fact that $\alpha$ and $\beta$ are the slope and intercept of the line that relates $\ln P/(1 - P)$, the log odds ratio, to $\theta$. In any range of $\theta$, the line is the same and hence $\alpha$ and $\beta$, and therefore $a$ and $b$, must be the same.

This example shows that, in contrast with the classical item difficulty and discrimination indices, the parameters of the item response model are invariant across ability subpopulations. We must, however, note several points in relation to the property of invariance. Referring back to Figure 2.5, we see that an exact relationship exists between the probabilities of success and the $\theta$ values. Furthermore, from Table 2.2 we see that at each $\theta$ level the observed probability of success (observed proportion correct on the item) is exactly equal to $P$; that is, *the model fits the data exactly in the population.* If the model does not fit the data *exactly* in the population, $\ln P/(1 - P)$ will not be an exact linear function of $\theta$, and, hence, different $\alpha$ and $\beta$ will be obtained when different sets of points are chosen. In other words, invariance only holds when the fit of the model to the data is exact in the population. This situation is identical to that in linear regression, where the regression coefficients are invariant only when the linear model fits the data exactly in the population.

A second point to be noted is that invariance is a property of the population. By definition, the item characteristic curve is the regression of item response on ability,

$$P = \mathcal{E}(U \mid \theta)$$

where $\mathcal{E}$ is the expected value. Hence, $P$ (for a given $\theta$) is the average of all item responses in the subpopulation of examinees with the specified ability value $\theta$. In the low-ability and high-ability subpopulations described in the example, the observed probability of success at each $\theta$ was exactly equal to $\mathcal{E}(U \mid \theta)$. Therefore, the exact linear relationship between $\ln P/(1 - P)$ and $\theta$ held; in other words, the invariance property was observed. On the other hand, if a sample is obtained from the subpopulation of examinees with the specified ability value $\theta$, it is extremely unlikely that the average of the item responses, or the observed probability of a correct response, will be exactly equal to $\mathcal{E}(U \mid \theta)$. Even if, by some chance, the observed probability was equal to $\mathcal{E}(U \mid \theta)$ at one value of $\theta$, it would almost never occur at all values of $\theta$. Hence, in samples, an exact linear relationship between $\ln P/(1 - P)$ and $\theta$ will not be observed. Therefore, we cannot expect to observe invariance, in the strict sense, in samples even when the model fits the data exactly in the population from which the sample has been drawn. This problem is further exacerbated by the errors introduced when the item and examinee parameters are estimated.

Nevertheless, it is important to determine whether invariance holds, since every application of item response theory capitalizes on this property. Although invariance is clearly an all-or-none property in the population and can never be observed in the strict sense, we can assess the "degree" to which it holds when we use samples of test data. For example, if two samples of different ability are drawn from the population and item parameters are estimated in each sample, the congruence between the two sets of estimates of each item parameter can be taken as an indication of the degree to which invariance holds. The degree of congruence can be assessed by examining the correlation between the two sets of estimates of each item parameter or by studying the corresponding scatterplot. Figure 2.6 shows a plot of the difficulty values for 75 items based on two samples from a population of examinees. Suppose that the samples differed with respect to ability. Since the difficulty estimates based on the two samples lie on a straight line, with some scatter, it can be concluded that the invariance property of item parameters holds. Some degree of scatter can be expected because of the use of samples; a large amount of scatter would indicate a lack of invariance that might be caused either by model-data misfit or poor item parameter estimation (which, unfortunately, are confounded).

The assessment of invariance described above is clearly subjective but is used because no objective criteria are currently available. Such investigations of the degree to which invariance holds are, as seen above, investigations of the fit of the model to the data, since invariance and model-data fit are equivalent concepts. This approach to assessing model-data fit is discussed in detail in chapter 4.

The discussion and example given above relate to the invariance of item parameters in different subpopulations of examinees. The invariance property also holds with respect to the ability parameters, meaning that the ability value of an examinee does not depend on the set of test items administered. To see this for the two-parameter model, we note that in the equation

$$\ln \frac{P}{1 - P} = Da(\theta - b)$$

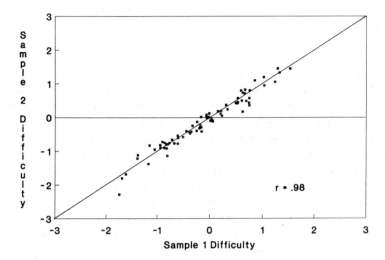

**Figure 2.6.** Plot of 3P Item Difficulty Values Based on Two Groups of Examinees

if we consider $a$ and $b$ to be variables, then the log odds ratio is a linear function of $a$ and $b$ with $\theta$ being the slope with respect to the variable $a$. As $a$ changes (as we consider items with different discrimination parameters), $\theta$ remains the same, showing that, no matter which items are used, the ability $\theta$ remains invariant. This is the same argument as was used to explain the invariance of item parameters.

The demonstration of invariance of item and ability parameters is obviously not restricted to the two-parameter model. Since the one-parameter model is a special case of the two-parameter model, at least mathematically, the ability and difficulty parameters will be invariant also for this model. For the three-parameter model the parameters $a$, $b$, and $c$ characterize the item response function. Since the mathematical form of the function remains the same no matter which range of $\theta$ is considered, the parameters that describe the function must be the same—invariant. A similar argument applies to $\theta$ as $a$, $b$, and $c$ vary.

The importance of the property of invariance of item and ability parameters cannot be overstated. This property is the cornerstone of item response theory and makes possible such important applications as equating, item banking, investigation of item bias, and adaptive testing.

## Other Promising Models

In addition to the one-, two-, and three-parameter logistic models, many other IRT models have been developed, including several models that can be applied to nondichotomous test data (see, for example, Andrich, 1978a, 1978b, 1978c, 1982; Masters, 1982; Masters & Wright, 1984; McDonald, 1989; Spray, 1990). For example, Bock (1972) developed a two-parameter logistic model that can be applied to *all* of the answer choices in a multiple-choice test item. The purpose of his *nominal response model* was to maximize the precision of ability estimates by using all the information contained in the examinees' responses, not just whether the item was answered correctly. Bock (1972) assumed that the probability that an examinee would select a particular item option $k$ (from $m$ available options) to item $i$ could be represented as

$$P_{ik}(\theta) = \frac{e^{a_{ik}^*(\theta - b_{ik}^*)}}{\sum\limits_{h=1}^{m} e^{a_{ih}^*(\theta - b_{ih}^*)}} \qquad i = 1, 2, \ldots, n; k = 1, 2, \ldots, m \quad [2.4]$$

At each $\theta$, the sum of probabilities across the $m$ options, $\sum_{k=1}^{m} P_{ik}$, is one. The quantities $(b_{ik}^*, a_{ik}^*)$ are item parameters related to the $k$th option. The model assumes no a priori ordering of the options.

The *graded response* model of Samejima (1969) assumes, in addition to the usual assumptions, that the available catagories to which an examinee responds can be ordered. Examples would include a 5-point Likert rating scale or, say, a 4-point rating scale for grading essays, or other scales representing levels of accomplishment or partial credit. This model, like the Bock model, attempts to obtain more information from examinees' responses than simply whether they give correct or incorrect answers. With the current interest in polytomous scoring models, Samejima's extension of the two-parameter logistic model to polytomous ordered categories is likely to receive increasing attention. (Also, see Masters & Wright, 1984, for various extensions of the one-parameter model to handle polytomous response data.)

Suppose the scoring categories for an item are arranged in order from low to high and denoted $x_i = 0, 1, \ldots, m_i$ where $(m_i + 1)$ is the number of scoring categories for the $i$th item. The probability of an examinee responding to an item in a particular category *or higher* can be given by a minor extension of the two-parameter logistic model:

$$P_{x_i}^*(\theta) = \frac{e^{Da_i(\theta - b_{x_i})}}{1 + e^{Da_i(\theta - b_{x_i})}} \qquad [2.5]$$

where $b_{x_i}$ is the "difficulty level" for category $m_i$. Other parameters in the model were defined earlier. With $(m_i + 1)$ categories, $m_i$ difficulty values need to be estimated for each item, plus one item discrimination parameter. The actual probability of an examinee receiving a score of $x_i$ is given by the expression

$$P_{x_i}(\theta) = P_{x_i}^*(\theta) - P_{x_i+1}^*(\theta) \qquad [2.6]$$

With, say, 50 items in a test, and a 5-point proficiency scale for each item, a total of $(50 \times 4) + 50 = 250$ item parameter values would need to be estimated.

The field of psychomotor assessment, too, has been influenced by item response models, and this influence has spawned new applications of relatively unknown IRT models (see Safrit, Costa, & Cohen, 1989; Spray, 1990). Instead of ability variables such as numerical ability and reading comprehension, variables such as physical fitness, basketball shooting ability, and abdominal strength are of interest in psychomotor assessment. In the simple binomial trials model, for example,

$$P(X = x \mid \theta) = \binom{n}{x} P(\theta)^x Q(\theta)^{n-x} \qquad [2.7]$$

where $P(X = x \mid \theta)$ represents the probability that an examinee completes $x$ of $n$ trials (e.g., shoots 8 out of 10 baskets). This probability could be represented by any of the logistic test models; however, the item parameters in the logistic model that would describe the trials, that is, items, would be equal for each trial, and, hence, item-parameter estimation would be considerably simplified. Trials would need to be independent and scored as pass or fail for this model to be applicable. If, for example, the binomial trials model is applied to basketball shooting data (e.g., number of successful shots), $\theta$ would be basketball shooting ability. As with all IRT applications, parameter invariance would be critical. Task (item) difficulty should be invariant across different groups of examinees, and abilities should be invariant across tasks that vary in difficulty.

Another IRT model that has been applied successfully is the Poisson counts model:

$$P(X = x \mid \theta, b) = \frac{e^{x(\theta - b)}}{x! e^{e^{(\theta - b)}}} \qquad [2.8]$$

where $x$ is the number of (say) sit-ups or push-ups completed in a minute and $b$ represents the difficulty of the task. These and other IRT models aimed at handling polytomous response data can be expected to receive increasing use in the future, as fewer assessments are based on dichotomously scored data.

## Exercises for Chapter 2

1. Item parameter values for six items are given in Table 2.3.

TABLE 2.3

| Item | $b$ | $a$ | $c$ |
|------|------|------|------|
| 1 | 1.0 | 1.8 | 0.00 |
| 2 | 1.0 | 0.7 | 0.00 |
| 3 | 1.0 | 1.8 | 0.25 |
| 4 | −0.5 | 1.2 | 0.20 |
| 5 | 0.5 | 1.2 | 0.00 |
| 6 | 0.0 | 0.5 | 0.10 |

a. For each item, compute $P(\theta)$ at $\theta = -3, -2, -1, 0, 1, 2,$ and 3. Plot the item characteristic curves.

b. Which item is the easiest?

c. Which item is the least discriminating?

d. Which item does an examinee with an ability of $\theta = 0$ have the highest probability of answering correctly? What is the examinee's probability of getting this item wrong?

2. Use the ICCs in Figure 2.4 to answer the following questions:

a. Which item is the easiest at $\theta = -1.0$?

b. Which item is the hardest at $\theta = 0.0$?

    c. Which two items are equally difficult at $\theta = -1.0$?

    d. Which item is most discriminating at $\theta = 2.0$?

3. Use the four two-parameter ICCs in Figure 2.3 to answer the following questions:

    a. What is the value of $P_3(\theta = -1.0)$?

    b. Which item is the least discriminating?

    c. How do the ICCs in Figure 2.3 differ from those in Figure 2.4?

4. For the three-parameter model, show that the probability of a correct response $P(\theta)$ at $\theta = b$ is

$$P(\theta) = \frac{1 + c}{2}$$

5. The probability of a correct response at certain values of $\theta$ for three items is given in Table 2.4.

**TABLE 2.4**

| $\theta$: | –3.0 | –2.5 | –2.0 | –1.5 | –1.0 | –0.5 | 0 | 0.5 | 1.0 | 1.5 | 2.0 | 2.5 | 3.0 |
|---|---|---|---|---|---|---|---|---|---|---|---|---|---|
| **Item** | | | | | | | | | | | | | |
| 1 | 0.01 | 0.01 | 0.02 | 0.04 | 0.07 | 0.13 | 0.22 | 0.35 | 0.50 | 0.65 | 0.78 | 0.87 | 0.93 |
| 2 | 0.00 | 0.00 | 0.01 | 0.04 | 0.11 | 0.26 | 0.50 | 0.74 | 0.89 | 0.96 | 0.99 | 0.99 | 0.99 |
| 3 | 0.20 | 0.20 | 0.20 | 0.20 | 0.20 | 0.21 | 0.23 | 0.26 | 0.32 | 0.44 | 0.60 | 0.76 | 0.88 |

Plot the ICCs for the three items.

    a. For Items 1 and 2, $c = 0$. Determine from the plot the $b$ values for these two items.

    b. For Item 3, $c = 0.2$. Determine from the plot the $b$ value for this item.

    c. How would you determine the $a$ value of an item from a plot of the ICC? Use this procedure to determine the $a$ value for each of the three items.

6. Responses of 40 examinees *at a given ability level* to two items are given in Table 2.5.

**TABLE 2.5**

| Item | Examinee Responses |
|---|---|
| 1 | 0 0 0 0 0 1 1 0 0 0 0 0 0 1 1 0 0 0 1 0 0 0 1 0 0 0 0 0 0 0 1 1 0 0 1 1 0 1 0 1 |
| 2 | 0 1 1 0 0 0 0 0 1 1 1 0 0 0 0 1 1 1 1 1 1 1 1 1 1 1 1 1 0 0 0 0 1 1 0 0 1 1 1 1 |

Construct a $2 \times 2$ table of correct and incorrect responses on the two items. Using a chi-square test for independence, determine if local independence holds for these two items at this ability level.

## Answers to Exercises for Chapter 2

1. a. See Table 2.6.

**TABLE 2.6**

| $\theta$ | $-3$ | $-2$ | $-1$ | $0$ | $1$ | $2$ | $3$ |
|---|---|---|---|---|---|---|---|
| Item |
| 1 | 0.000 | 0.000 | 0.002 | 0.045 | 0.500 | 0.955 | 0.998 |
| 2 | 0.008 | 0.027 | 0.085 | 0.233 | 0.500 | 0.767 | 0.915 |
| 3 | 0.250 | 0.250 | 0.252 | 0.284 | 0.625 | 0.966 | 0.998 |
| 4 | 0.205 | 0.236 | 0.412 | 0.788 | 0.964 | 0.995 | 0.999 |
| 5 | 0.000 | 0.006 | 0.045 | 0.265 | 0.735 | 0.955 | 0.994 |
| 6 | 0.165 | 0.239 | 0.369 | 0.550 | 0.731 | 0.861 | 0.935 |

   b. Item 4. c. Item 6. d. Item 4. $P(\text{failure}) = 1 - P(\theta) = 1 - 0.788 = 0.212$.
2. a. Item 4. b. Item 1. c. Items 5 and 6. d. Item 2.
3. a. Approximately 0.50. b. Item 2. c. In Figure 2.3, the lower asymptotes of the ICCs are all zero; in Figure 2.4, the lower asymptotes of the ICCs are not all zero.
4. $P(\theta = b) = c + (1 - c) / [1 + e^{-Da(b-b)}]$
   $$= c + (1 - c) / (1 + e^{0})$$
   $$= c + (1 - c) / (1 + 1)$$
   $$= c + (1 - c) / 2$$
   $$= (2c + 1 - c) / 2$$
   $$= (1 + c) / 2$$
5. a. Item 1: $b = 1.0$. Item 2: $b = 0.0$
   b. $(1 + c) / 2 = (1 + 0.2) / 2 = 0.6$
   $b = \theta$ value at which $P(\theta) = 0.6$; $b = 2.0$
   c. $a = $ slope of ICC at $b$.
   Draw the tangent to the curve at $\theta = b$ and determine its slope by taking any two points on the tangent and dividing the $y$ increment by the $x$ increment.
6. See Table 2.7.

**TABLE 2.7**

|  |  | Item 2 Incorrect | Item 2 Correct |  |
|---|---|---|---|---|
| Item 1 | Incorrect | 8 (A) | 20 (B) | 28 |
|  | Correct | 8 (C) | 4 (D) | 12 |
|  |  | 16 | 24 | 40 |

$$\chi^2 = N\,(AD - BC)^2 / (A + B)(B + D)(D + C)(C + A)$$

$$= 40(8 \times 4 - 20 \times 8)^2 / (8 + 20)(20 + 4)(4 + 8)(8 + 8)$$

$$= 5.08 > \chi^2_{1,.05}$$

Since the computed $\chi^2$ exceeds the tabulated value, we can reject the hypothesis of independence. Local independence does not hold at this ability level. We would, therefore, conclude that a unidimensional model does not fit the data.

## Note

1. For convenience, $P(U_i \mid \theta)$ will be written as $P_i(\theta)$; this notation will be used in specifying item characteristic functions.

# 3

# Ability and Item Parameter Estimation

The first and most important step in applying item response theory to test data is that of estimating the parameters that characterize the chosen item response model. In fact, the successful application of item response theory hinges on the availability of satisfactory procedures for estimating the parameters of the model.

In item response models, the probability of a correct response depends on the examinee's ability, $\theta$, and the parameters that characterize the item. Both ability and item parameters are unknown; what is known are the responses of the examinees to the test items. The problem of estimation is to determine the value of $\theta$ for each examinee and the item parameters from the item responses. This problem is similar to that encountered in regression analysis where, from observed responses to a variable, the parameters that characterize the regression model—the regression coefficients—must be estimated.

Two major differences distinguish regression models and item response models. First, the regression model is usually linear, while item response models are nonlinear. Second, and most important, the regressor (independent) variable in regression analysis is observable; that is, scores on this variable can be observed. In item response models the "regressor variable" $\theta$ is unobservable. If $\theta$ were observable or known, the problem of estimation of item parameters, or the "regression coefficients," would simplify considerably, although we would still be dealing with a nonlinear regression model. Similarly, if the item parameters are known, the estimation of ability is reasonably straightforward.

Estimation of parameters can be accomplished in several ways. In the unlikely event that the model fits the data exactly, and when $\theta$ is known, the procedure demonstrated in the section on parameter invariance could be used. In this case, only as many points as there are item parameters in the model are needed to solve for the unknown parameters. When a sample is obtained, the above procedure cannot be used because the model will not fit the data exactly. In this case, our strategy is to find the parameter values that will produce the "best fitting" curve. In linear regression, best fit is defined often in terms of the least squares criterion. In IRT models the least squares criterion is not used because it is difficult to determine the properties of least squares estimates in nonlinear models. Alternatively, the parameters could be estimated using a maximum likelihood criterion. The sampling distributions of maximum likelihood estimates are known in large samples, and this information can be used in a variety of ways in IRT applications. We shall first describe the maximum likelihood procedure for estimating ability when the item parameters are known, and then describe the procedures for estimating item parameters.

### Estimation of Ability

Suppose that a randomly chosen examinee responds to a set of $n$ items with response pattern $(U_1, U_2, \ldots, U_j, \ldots, U_n)$ where $U_j$ is either 1 (a correct response) or 0 (an incorrect response) on item $j$. By the assumption of local independence, the joint probability of observing the response pattern is the product of the probabilities of observing each item response, that is,

$$P(U_1, U_2, \ldots, U_j, \ldots, U_n \mid \theta) =$$
$$P(U_1 \mid \theta) P(U_2 \mid \theta) \ldots P(U_j \mid \theta) \ldots P(U_n \mid \theta),$$

which may be expressed more compactly as

$$P(U_1, U_2, \ldots, U_n \mid \theta) = \prod_{j=1}^{n} P(U_j \mid \theta)$$

Since $U_j$ is either 1 or 0, this can be taken into account by writing the likelihood function as

$$P(U_1, U_2, \ldots, U_n \mid \theta) = \prod_{j=1}^{n} P(U_j \mid \theta)^{U_j} [1 - P(U_j \mid \theta)]^{1 - U_j}$$

or simply as

$$P(U_1, U_2, \ldots, U_n \mid \theta) = \prod_{j=1}^{n} P_j^{U_j} Q_j^{1-U_j} \qquad [3.1]$$

where $P_j = P(U_j \mid \theta)$ and $Q_j = 1 - P(U_j \mid \theta)$.

Equation 3.1 is an expression of the joint probability of a response pattern. When the response pattern is observed, $U_j = u_j$, the probabilistic interpretation is no longer appropriate; the expression for the joint probability is now called the *likelihood function* and is denoted as $L(u_1, u_2, \ldots, u_j, \ldots, u_n \mid \theta)$ where $u_j$ is the observed response to item $j$. Thus,

$$L(u_1, u_2, \ldots, u_n \mid \theta) = \prod_{j=1}^{n} P_j^{u_j} Q_j^{1-u_j} \qquad [3.2]$$

Since $P_j$ and $Q_j$ are functions of $\theta$ and the item parameters, the likelihood function is also a function of these parameters.

As an example, consider the responses of five examinees to five items with known item parameter values, given in Table 3.1. The likelihood function for any examinee may be written using the general expression above. For Examinee 3, for example, $u_1 = 0, u_2 = 0, u_3 = 0, u_4 = 1, u_5 = 1$. Hence, the likelihood function for this examinee is

$$L(u_1, u_2, u_3, u_4, u_5 \mid \theta) = (P_1^0 Q_1^1)(P_2^0 Q_2^1)(P_3^0 Q_3^1)(P_4^1 Q_4^0)(P_5^1 Q_5^0)$$

$$= Q_1 Q_2 Q_3 P_4 P_5$$

Since $P$ (and hence $Q$) are item response functions whose forms depend on the item parameters, and the item parameters are known in this example, the exact values of the likelihood function for a given $\theta$ can be computed. In particular, a graph of the likelihood function as $\theta$ varies can be plotted. Since the likelihood function is a product of quantities, each bounded between 0 and 1, its value will be very small. A better scaling of the likelihood function can be obtained by transforming it using logarithms. Furthermore, because of the following properties of logarithms,

$$\ln xy = \ln x + \ln y$$

**TABLE 3.1** Item Parameters and Response Patterns for Five Examinees on Five Test Items

| Item | Item Parameters | | | Examinee Item Responses | | | | |
|------|------|------|------|---|---|---|---|---|
| | $a_i$ | $b_i$ | $c_i$ | 1 | 2 | 3 | 4 | 5 |
| 1 | 1.27 | 1.19 | 0.10 | 1 | 1 | 0 | 0 | 0 |
| 2 | 1.34 | 0.59 | 0.15 | 1 | 0 | 0 | 1 | 0 |
| 3 | 1.14 | 0.15 | 0.15 | 1 | 1 | 0 | 1 | 0 |
| 4 | 1.00 | −0.59 | 0.20 | 0 | 0 | 1 | 1 | 0 |
| 5 | 0.67 | −2.00 | 0.01 | 0 | 0 | 1 | 1 | 1 |

and

$$\ln x^a = a \ln x$$

using logarithms simplifies the computations (and, as we shall see, computation of the first derivative) considerably. Using the above two properties, the general expression for the logarithm of the likelihood function (log-likelihood, for short) may be written as

$$\ln L(\boldsymbol{u} \mid \theta) = \sum_{j=1}^{n} [u_j \ln P_j + (1 - u_j) \ln (1 - P_j)]$$

Here, $\boldsymbol{u}$ is the vector of item responses. Graphs of the logarithms of the likelihood for Examinees 3, 4, and 5 are given in Figure 3.1. The log-likelihood for Examinee 3 peaks at $\theta = -0.5$, while for Examinee 4 the log-likelihood peaks at $\theta = 1$. For Examinee 5 the peak is at $\theta = -1.5$. The value of $\theta$ that makes the likelihood function (or, correspondingly, the log-likelihood) for an examinee a maximum is defined as the *maximum likelihood estimate* of $\theta$ for that examinee.

The problem of finding the maximum value of a function is not a trivial one. The graphical procedure described above was used for illustration and is not feasible when many examinees and many items are used. The value that maximizes the function may be found using a search procedure with a computer. More efficient procedures use the fact that, at the point where the function reaches a maximum, the slope of the function (the first derivative) is zero. Thus, the maximum likelihood estimate may be determined by solving the equation obtained by

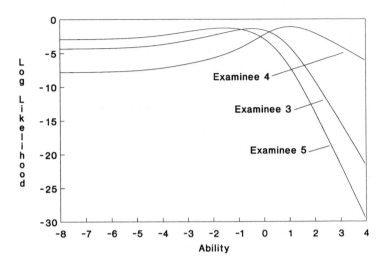

**Figure 3.1.** Log-Likelihood Functions for Three Examinees

setting the first derivative of the likelihood or log-likelihood function equal to zero. Again, this equation cannot be solved directly, and approximation methods must be used. The most popular of the approximation methods is the Newton–Raphson procedure described in detail in Hambleton and Swaminathan (1985).

Unfortunately, the likelihood (or log-likelihood) function might not have a finite value as its maximum, as when an examinee answers all items correctly or all items incorrectly. In this case, the maximum likelihood estimate will be $\theta = +\infty$ or $\theta = -\infty$. Some peculiar response patterns (which cannot be discerned as such a priori) may result also in likelihood functions that do not have a finite absolute maximum. The log-likelihood functions for the first two examinees from Table 3.1 are shown in Figure 3.2. For Examinee 2, the log-likelihood function appears to have a maximum at the point $\theta = 0.9$; however, the function has a higher value at $\theta = -\infty$ (values of the function are shown in the figure only to $\theta = -6$). For Examinee 1, too, the maximum likelihood function has its maximum at $\theta = -\infty$. Hence, for both examinees, maximum likelihood estimates do not exist. The reason for this situation is that the response patterns of these two examinees are aberrant: The

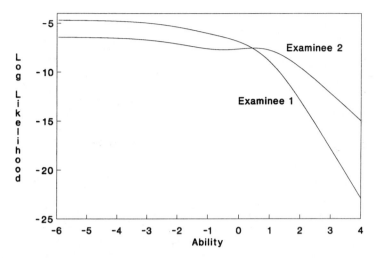

**Figure 3.2.** Log-Likelihood Functions for Two Examinees with Aberrant Responses

examinees answered some relatively difficult and discriminating items correctly and answered some of the easier items incorrectly. In cases like this the numerical procedures used to find the maximum usually will diverge. The problem noted above with aberrant responses occurs only with the three-parameter model and not with the one- or two-parameter models (see Hambleton & Swaminathan [1985], and Yen, Burket, & Sykes [in press] for discussions of this issue), and may occur even for tests with as many as 40 items.

The maximum likelihood estimates (MLEs), when they exist, have well-known asymptotic (i.e., large sample) properties. Since we are dealing with an examinee, *asymptotic* refers to increasing test length. As test length increases, the MLE of $\theta$, denoted as $\hat{\theta}$, is distributed normally with mean $\theta$. This implies that the asymptotic distribution of $\hat{\theta}$ is centered on the true value of $\theta$; hence, the MLE $\hat{\theta}$ is unbiased in long tests. The standard deviation of $\hat{\theta}$, or the standard error, denoted as $SE(\hat{\theta})$, is a function of $\theta$ and is given as

$$SE(\hat{\theta}) = \frac{1}{\sqrt{I(\theta)}}$$

where $I(\theta)$ is what is called the *information function*. Since $\theta$ is not known, the information function must be computed by substituting $\hat{\theta}$ for $\theta$ in the above expression. Computation of the information function, its properties, and its role in test construction are described in detail in chapter 6.

The normality of $\hat{\theta}$ can be used to construct a confidence interval for $\theta$. The $(1 - \alpha)\%$ confidence interval for $\theta$ is given by

$$( \hat{\theta} - z_{\alpha/2} \text{ SE} (\hat{\theta}), \ \hat{\theta} + z_{\alpha/2} \text{ SE} (\hat{\theta}) )$$

where $\text{SE} (\hat{\theta})$ is the standard error evaluated at $\hat{\theta}$, and $z_{\alpha/2}$ is the upper $(1 - \alpha/2)$ percentile point of the normal distribution. For the 95% confidence interval, $\alpha = 0.05$ and $z_{\alpha/2} = 1.96$.

The problem of not finding maximum likelihood estimates in some situations can be overcome if a Bayesian estimation procedure is used. The basic idea is to modify the likelihood function to incorporate any prior information we may have about the ability parameters. For example, we may be able to say, based on some previous experience, that $\theta$ is distributed normally with mean $\mu$ and standard deviation $\sigma$. In this case, the prior information can be expressed in the form of a density function and denoted as $f(\theta)$.

Bayes' theorem states that the probability of an event A given B is

$$P(A \mid B) \propto P(B \mid A) P(A)$$

where $P(A)$ is the prior probability of event A occurring. The above relationship is also true for density functions, where A is $\theta$ and B is the observed item response pattern, *u*. Bayes' theorem can be written then as

$$f(\theta \mid u) \propto f(u \mid \theta) f(\theta)$$

Now, $f(u \mid \theta)$ is, in fact, the likelihood function and, hence,

$$f(\theta \mid u) \propto L(u \mid \theta) f(\theta)$$

The revised likelihood function $f(\theta \mid u)$ is called the posterior density and its mode is the "most probable" value for $\theta$, and can be taken as an estimate of θ. Note that if we assume a uniform prior distribution for θ (i.e., $f(\theta) = k$, a constant) then

$$f(\theta \mid \boldsymbol{u}) \propto L(\boldsymbol{u} \mid \theta)$$

In this case the Bayesian estimate is *numerically* identical to the maximum likelihood estimate. We emphasize numerically because the philosophical basis underlying the Bayesian procedure is very different from the classical or relative frequency notion of probability (see Kendall & Stuart [1961] for details on this issue). Using a Bayesian approach solves some of the difficulties encountered with the maximum likelihood approach. Bayesian estimates of θ can be obtained for zero items correct and perfect response patterns, and for "aberrant" response patterns.

The posterior distribution of θ may be described in many ways. The mode of the distribution, the Bayesian modal estimate, provides only one description. The mean of the distribution also may be used as an estimate. The mean can be computed by approximating the posterior distribution of θ in a finite interval with a histogram, that is, forming a frequency distribution with $k$ values of θ. The frequency at the point $\theta_j$ $(j = 1, \ldots, k)$ is $f(\theta_j \mid \boldsymbol{u})$. The mean can then be obtained in the usual way:

$$\mu(\theta \mid \boldsymbol{u}) = \frac{\displaystyle\sum_{j=1}^{k} \theta_j f(\theta_j \mid \boldsymbol{u})}{\displaystyle\sum_{j=1}^{k} f(\theta_j \mid \boldsymbol{u})} \qquad [3.3]$$

Bock and Mislevy (1982) have called this estimate the *Expected A Posteriori* (EAP) estimate.

## Estimation of Item Parameters

In describing the procedures for estimating θ, we assumed that the item parameters were known. At some point, we have to face the fact that the item parameters also must be estimated! For estimating the ability of an examinee when item parameters are known, we administer many items to the examinee and obtain the likelihood function for the responses of the examinee to $n$ items. Conversely, if we want to estimate item parameters when $\theta$ is known for each examinee, we administer the item of interest to many examinees and obtain the likelihood function for the responses of $N$ examinees to the item, that is,

$$L(u_1, u_2, \ldots, u_N \mid \theta, a, b, c) = \prod_{i=1}^{N} P_i^{u_i} Q_i^{1-u_i}$$

where $a$, $b$, and $c$ are the item parameters (assuming a three-parameter model).

The difference between the likelihood function for an examinee and that for an item is that, for an item, the assumption of local independence need not be invoked; we merely assume that the responses of $N$ examinees to an item are independent, a standard assumption in statistics. The assumption of local independence is more stringent in that we must assume that the responses of an examinee to two or more items are independent.

When the $\theta$ values are known, the estimation of item parameters is straightforward and is comparable to the procedure described in the previous section. The difference is that the likelihood function for an item, unlike that for an examinee, is multidimensional for the item parameters; that is, it is a function of three parameters. Thus, to find the MLE of the parameters $a$, $b$, and $c$, we must find the values of $a$, $b$, and $c$ that correspond to the maximum value of a surface in three dimensions. This is accomplished by finding the first derivative of the likelihood function with respect to each of the parameters $a$, $b$, and $c$, setting these derivatives to zero, and solving simultaneously the resulting system of nonlinear equations in three unknowns. Obviously, we solve for two unknowns when the two-parameter model is used, and solve for only one unknown when the one-parameter model is used. Again, the Newton–Raphson procedure, in its multivariate form, is used commonly to solve these equations. When the ability of each examinee is known, each item may be considered separately without reference to the other items. Thus, the estimation procedure must be repeated $n$ times, once for each item.

## Joint Estimation of Item and Ability Parameters

It is apparent that at some point neither $\theta$ nor the item parameters will be known. This is the most common situation and presents the most difficult problem. In this case the responses of all the examinees to all the items must be considered simultaneously.

The likelihood function when $N$ examinees respond to $n$ items, using the assumption of local independence, is

$$L(u_1, u_2, \ldots, u_N \mid \theta, \boldsymbol{a}, \boldsymbol{b}, \boldsymbol{c}) = \prod_{i=1}^{N} \prod_{j=1}^{n} P_{ij}^{u_{ij}} \, Q_{ij}^{1-u_{ij}}$$

where $u_i$ is the response pattern of examinee $i$ to $n$ items; $\theta$ is the vector of $N$ ability parameters; $\boldsymbol{a}, \boldsymbol{b},$ and $\boldsymbol{c}$ are the vectors of item parameters for the $n$-item test. The number of item parameters is $3n$ in the three-parameter model ($2n$ for the two- and $n$ for the one-parameter model, respectively). Local independence must be assumed since $\theta$s are not known. The number of ability parameters is $N$ and, hence, for the three-parameter model a total of $3n + N$ parameters is to be estimated. Before the estimation can proceed, however, the problem of indeterminacy must be addressed.

In the likelihood function given above, the item and ability parameters are not uniquely determined. In the item response function for, say, the three-parameter model (see Equation 2.3), if we replace $\theta$ by $\theta^* = \alpha\theta + \beta$, $b$ by $b^* = \alpha b + \beta$, and $a$ by $a^* = a/\alpha$, the probability of a correct response remains unchanged,

$$P(\theta) = P(\theta^*)$$

Since $\alpha$ and $\beta$ are arbitrary scaling constants, the likelihood function will not have a unique maximum. Any numerical procedure employed to find the maximum of the likelihood function will fail because of this indeterminacy. This problem does not arise in the estimation of $\theta$ when item parameters are known or in the parallel situation in which item parameters are estimated in the presence of known ability parameters, because there is no indeterminacy in these situations.

The problem of indeterminacy may be eliminated by choosing an arbitrary scale for the ability values (or the $b$ values); usually, the mean and standard deviation of the $N$ ability values (or the $n$ item difficulty values) are set to be 0 and 1, respectively. As we shall see later, this scaling must be taken into account when comparing estimates of item parameters for two or more groups.

Once the indeterminacy is eliminated, the values of the item and ability parameters that maximize the likelihood function can be determined. In the simultaneous or *joint maximum likelihood estimation* procedure, this determination must be done in two stages. In the first stage, initial values for the ability parameters are chosen. The logarithm of the ratio of number-right score to number-wrong score for each examinee provides good starting values. These values are then standardized (to eliminate the indeterminacy) and, treating the ability values as known, the item parameters are estimated. In the second stage, treating the item parameters as known, the ability parameters are estimated. This procedure is repeated until the values of the estimates do not change between two successive estimation stages. This joint maximum likelihood procedure is implemented in LOGIST (Wingersky, 1983) for the one-, two-, and three-parameter models, and in BICAL (Wright, Mead, & Bell, 1979) and BIGSCALE (Wright, Schulz, & Linacre, 1989) for the one-parameter model.

The joint maximum likelihood procedure, while conceptually appealing, has some disadvantages. First, ability estimates with perfect and zero scores do not exist. Second, item parameter estimates for items that are answered correctly (or incorrectly) by all examinees do not exist. Items and examinees exhibiting these patterns must be eliminated before estimation can proceed. Third, in the two- and three-parameter models the joint maximum likelihood procedure does not yield consistent estimates of item and ability parameters. (Swaminathan & Gifford [1983] have shown empirically that consistent estimates may be obtained for item and ability parameters if both the number of examinees and the number of items become large.) Fourth, in the three-parameter model, unless restrictions are placed on the values the item and ability parameters take, the numerical procedure for finding the estimates may fail.

Alternative approaches to estimation are available. One approach is to obtain Bayesian estimates of the parameters using prior distributions. Swaminathan and Gifford (1982, 1985, 1986) have developed Bayesian procedures for the one-, two-, and three-parameter models in which prior distributions are placed on the item and ability parameters. This procedure eliminates the problems encountered in the joint maximum likelihood procedure, namely that of improper estimates for certain response patterns.

The problem of inconsistent joint maximum likelihood estimates occurs because both the item and ability parameters are estimated simultaneously. This problem disappears if the item parameters can be estimated without any reference to the ability parameters. If we consider the examinees as having been selected randomly from a population, then, by specifying a distribution for the ability parameters, we can integrate them out of the likelihood function (integrating out the ability parameters has the same effect as "running" over the ability distribution to obtain a marginal likelihood function in terms of the item parameters). The resulting "marginal maximum likelihood estimates" do have desirable asymptotic properties; that is, the item parameter estimates are consistent as the number of examinees increases. This marginal maximum likelihood estimation procedure was developed by Bock and Lieberman (1970), refined by Bock and Aitkin (1981), and implemented in the computer program BILOG by Mislevy and Bock (1984). The marginal maximum likelihood procedure is computationally more intensive than the joint maximum likelihood procedure because of the integration that is required. Moreover, in order to obtain the marginal likelihood function of the item parameters, it is necessary to approximate the distribution of ability. For a good approximation of the ability distribution, the availability of a large number of examinees is important. Hence, the marginal maximum likelihood procedure should be carried out only with sufficiently large numbers of examinees.

Once the item parameters have been estimated using the marginal maximum likelihood procedure, the item parameter estimates may be treated as known and the abilities of the examinees can be estimated using the method outlined earlier in this chapter. Again, the larger the number of items, the better the ability parameter estimates. Either the maximum likelihood estimates of ability or, if desired, the EAP estimates of ability may be obtained.

In some situations, even the marginal maximum likelihood procedure may fail; that is, the numerical procedure may fail to yield a satisfactory result even after a large number of iterations. This failure happens primarily in the estimation of the $c$ parameter in the three-parameter model. Poor estimates of $c$, in turn, degrade estimates of other item parameters and of ability (Swaminathan & Gifford, 1985). Bayesian estimation (Mislevy, 1986) solves this problem (in fact, within the BILOG computer program, a prior distribution is placed on the $c$ parameter values as the default option).

## Standard Errors of Item Parameter Estimates

The concept of the information function, briefly introduced earlier, is a generic concept that relates to the variance of a maximum likelihood estimator. When the maximum likelihood estimate of the ability parameter is obtained, its variance is given as the reciprocal of the corresponding information function. Similarly, when maximum likelihood estimates of item parameters are obtained, the *variance–covariance matrix* of the estimates is given as the inverse of the *information matrix* of item parameter estimates (since, in the case of the two- and three-parameter models, each item is characterized by two and three parameters, respectively). The elements of the information matrix for the joint maximum likelihood estimates for each item are arranged in the following manner (since the matrix is symmetric, only the upper triangle elements are given):

$$I_i = \begin{bmatrix} I_{aai} & I_{abi} & I_{aci} \\ & I_{bbi} & I_{bci} \\ & & I_{cci} \end{bmatrix} \qquad i = 1, 2, \ldots, n$$

The expressions for the elements are given below (Hambleton & Swaminathan, 1985; Lord, 1980).

$$I_{aai} = \frac{D^2}{(1 - c_i)^2} \sum_{j=1}^{N} (\theta_j - b_i)^2 (P_{ij} - c_i)^2 \frac{Q_{ij}}{P_{ij}}$$

$$I_{abi} = -\frac{D^2 a_i}{(1 - c_i)^2} \sum_{j=1}^{N} (\theta_j - b_i) (P_{ij} - c_i)^2 \frac{Q_{ij}}{P_{ij}}$$

$$I_{aci} = \frac{D}{(1 - c_i)^2} \sum_{j=1}^{N} (\theta_j - b_i) (P_{ij} - c_i) \frac{Q_{ij}}{P_{ij}}$$

$$I_{bbi} = \frac{D^2 a_i^2}{(1 - c_i)^2} \sum_{j=1}^{N} (P_{ij} - c_i)^2 \frac{Q_{ij}}{P_{ij}}$$

$$I_{bci} = -\frac{D a_i}{(1 - c_i)^2} \sum_{j=1}^{N} (P_{ij} - c_i) \frac{Q_{ij}}{P_{ij}}$$

$$I_{cci} = \frac{1}{(1 - c_i)^2} \sum_{j=1}^{N} \frac{Q_{ij}}{P_{ij}}$$

Simple expressions for the variance–covariance matrix of marginal maximum likelihood estimates are not available, but a description of the procedure for obtaining them is given in Mislevy and Bock (1984) and Mislevy (1986). The variance–covariance matrix of the item parameter estimates is important when comparing the item parameters in two groups, a problem that arises in bias or differential item functioning studies (Lord, 1980).

## Summary of Parameter Estimation Methods

In the preceding sections, maximum likelihood, marginal maximum likelihood, and Bayesian estimation procedures were described. These are the most widely used estimation procedures. For reviews of current procedures, refer to Baker (1987) and Swaminathan (1983). Several other approaches to estimation were not described in this chapter. A list of the available estimation procedures with brief descriptions is given below.

- *Joint maximum likelihood procedure* (Lord, 1974, 1980), applicable to the one-, two-, and three-parameter models. The ability and item parameters are estimated simultaneously.
- *Marginal maximum likelihood procedure* (Bock & Aitkin, 1981), applicable to the one-, two-, and three-parameter models. The ability parameters are integrated out, and the item parameters are estimated. With the item parameter estimates determined, the ability parameters are estimated.
- *Conditional maximum likelihood procedure* (Andersen, 1972, 1973; Rasch, 1960), applicable only to the one-parameter model. Here, the likelihood function is conditioned on the number right score.
- *Joint and marginal Bayesian estimation procedures* (Mislevy, 1986; Swaminathan & Gifford, 1982, 1985, 1986), applicable to the one-, two-, and three-parameter models. Prior distributions are placed on the item and ability parameters, eliminating some of the problems, such as improper estimation of parameters and nonconvergence, encountered with joint and marginal maximum likelihood procedures.
- *Heuristic estimation procedure* (Urry, 1974, 1978), applicable primarily to the two- and three-parameter models.
- *Method based on nonlinear factor analysis procedures* (McDonald, 1967, 1989), applicable to the two-parameter and a modified case of the three-parameter model in which the $c$-values are fixed.

In addition, when item parameters are known, estimation of ability can be carried out by obtaining the mode of the likelihood function, or, in the case of Bayesian procedures, either the mean or the mode of the posterior density function of $\theta$. The procedures summarized above are implemented in computer programs described in the next section.

## Computer Programs for Parameter Estimation

Until recently, few computer programs were available for estimation of the parameters of the IRT models introduced earlier. In the 1970s the most widely known and used programs were BICAL (Wright et al., 1979) and LOGIST (Wingersky, Barton, & Lord, 1982). BICAL fits the one-parameter model; LOGIST fits the one-, two-, and three-parameter models. Both programs use joint maximum likelihood estimation procedures, and both remain widely used. LOGIST remains the standard by which new estimation programs are judged.

Other programs available in the 1970s were PML (Gustafsson, 1980a) and ANCILLES (Urry, 1974, 1978). PML fits the one-parameter model using the conditional maximum likelihood procedure, while ANCILLES fits the three-parameter model using an heuristic procedure. PML has not been used widely in the United States, and ANCILLES is not used often because its estimation procedure is not well grounded theoretically and other programs have been shown to produce better estimates.

In the 1980s several new estimation programs were introduced. Most notable of these were BILOG (Mislevy & Bock, 1984) and ASCAL (Assessment Systems Corporation, 1988). BILOG fits the one-, two-, and three-parameter models using marginal maximum likelihood procedures with optional Bayesian procedures; ASCAL fits the three-parameter model using Bayesian procedures. BILOG is available in both mainframe and microcomputer versions, while ASCAL is a microcomputer program.

Also available in the early 1980s was the program NOHARM (Fraser & McDonald, 1988), which fits two- and three-parameter models (with fixed $c$-values) using a nonlinear factor analysis approach. NOHARM has not received much attention in the United States.

Other developments included microcomputer programs for fitting the one-parameter model, MICROSCALE (Mediax Interactive Technologies, 1986) and RASCAL (Assessment Systems Corporation, 1988). A microcomputer version of LOGIST is being developed and is expected to be released in 1991 or 1992. RIDA (Glas, 1990) is a new microcomputer program for analyzing dichotomous data using the one-parameter model. Both marginal and conditional maximum likelihood estimation procedures are available. A special feature is the capability of analyzing various incomplete test designs that often arise in test equating (see chapter 9).

Most recently, interest in IRT programs that handle polytomous data (Thissen, 1986; Wright et al., 1989) and multidimensional data (Carlson, 1987) has developed, but work on the latter topic is only just beginning and considerable amounts of research are needed before Carlson's program can be used operationally. A summary of the programs listed above and their advantages and key features is given in Table 3.2. Sources for the programs are listed in Appendix B.

**TABLE 3.2** Currently Available IRT Parameter Estimation Programs

| Program | Source | Model | Estimation Procedure | Computer Requirements | Pros (+), Cons (−), and Features (*) |
|---------|--------|-------|----------------------|----------------------|--------------------------------------|
| BICAL (Replaced by BIG-SCALE) | Wright et al. (1979); Wright et al. (1989) | 1P | Unconditional Maximum Likelihood | Most mainframes | + Inexpensive<br>+ Gives standard errors<br>+ Gives graphical/ statistical fit analysis |
| MICRO-SCALE | Mediax Interactive Technologies (1986) | 1P Multi-category | Unconditional Maximum Likelihood | PC | * PC version of BICAL<br>* Data can be input in a spreadsheet |
| PML | Gustafsson (1980a) | 1P | Conditional Maximum Likelihood | Unknown | + Estimates are consistent<br>− Computationally intensive<br>* Not widely used in the U.S. |
| RASCAL | Assessment Systems Corp. (1988) | 1P | Unconditional Maximum Likelihood | PC | + Includes analyses of fit<br>* Incorporated in the Micro-CAT package |
| RIDA | Glas (1990) | 1P | Conditional or Marginal Maximum Likelihood | PC | + Provides a complete analysis of examinees and items<br>+ Handles incomplete designs for test equating<br>+ Includes fit analysis |

**TABLE 3.2** (Continued)

| Program | Source | Model | Estimation Procedure | Computer Requirements | Pros (+), Cons (−), and Features (*) |
|---------|--------|-------|---------------------|----------------------|--------------------------------------|
| ANCILLES | Urry (1974, 1978) | 3P | Heuristic | Most mainframes | + Inexpensive<br>− Often deletes items/ examinees<br>− Estimation procedure not well grounded theoretically<br>* Not widely used |
| ASCAL | Assessment Systems Corp. (1988) | 1P 2P 3P | Modified Bayesian | PC | + Includes analysis of fit<br>+ Incorporated in the Micro-CAT package<br>* Uses Bayesian procedures |
| LOGIST | Wingersky (1983); Wingersky et al. (1982) | 1P 2P 3P | Unconditional Maximum Likelihood | IBM/CDC Mainframes (Version IV) | + LOGIST V gives standard errors<br>+ Flexible, many options<br>+ Allows omits/ not reached<br>− Input specifications are complex<br>− Expensive to run<br>− Difficult to convert for non-IBM equipment<br>− Places many constraints on the parameters to obtain convergence |

*(Continued)*

**TABLE 3.2** (Continued)

| Program | Source | Model | Estimation Procedure | Computer Requirements | Pros (+), Cons (−), and Features (*) |
|---------|--------|-------|----------------------|----------------------|--------------------------------------|
| BILOG | Mislevy & Bock (1984) | 1P 2P 3P | Marginal Maximum Likelihood | IBM mainframe PC Version | + Optional Bayes's estimates<br>+ Priors prevent extreme estimates<br>− Expensive to run on main-frame<br>− Wrong priors may give bad estimates |
| NOHARM | Fraser & McDonald (1988) | 1P 2P 3P | Least Squares | Most mainframes PC | + Fits a multi-dimensional model<br>+ Includes residual analysis<br>− $c$ parameter is fixed<br>* Not widely used in the U.S. |
| MULTILOG | Thissen (1986) | Multi-category | | IBM mainframe | * Generalization of BILOG to handle multi-category data |
| MIRTE | Carlson (1987) | 1P 2P 3P | Unconditional Maximum Likelihood | IBM mainframe PC | + Fits a multi-dimensional model<br>+ Gives stan-dard errors<br>+ Includes residual analysis<br>− $c$ parameter is fixed |

## Exercises for Chapter 3

1. For the five items given in Table 3.1, the responses of an examinee are [0 0 0 1 1].

   a. What is the likelihood function for this examinee? State the assumption that must be made in determining the likelihood function.

   b. Plot the likelihood function at $\theta$ values from $-1$ to $0$ in increments of 0.1. Based on the graph, determine the maximum likelihood estimate of $\theta$.

2. The item parameters (obtained using a two-parameter model) for four items are given in Table 3.3.

**TABLE 3.3**

| Item | b | a |
|------|-----|-----|
| 1 | 0.0 | 1.0 |
| 2 | 1.0 | 1.0 |
| 3 | 1.0 | 2.0 |
| 4 | 1.5 | 2.0 |

The maximum likelihood estimate of an examinee who takes this four-item test is 1.5.

   a. Determine the standard error of the estimate.

   b. Construct a 95% confidence interval for $\theta$.

3. Consider three examinees with ability values $\theta = -1, 0, 1$. The responses of the three examinees to an item are 0, 0, 1, respectively. Assume that the one-parameter model with a certain (unknown) $b$ value fits the item.

   a. Write down the likelihood function in terms of the unknown $b$ value, and state the assumptions that are made.

   b. Plot the likelihood function at $b$ values of 0 to 1 in increments of 0.1. Based on the plot, determine the maximum likelihood estimate of $b$.

4. a. For the one-parameter model, write down the information and standard error of the item difficulty estimate.

   b. Compute the standard error of the difficulty parameter estimate for the data given in Exercise 3.

## Answers to Exercises for Chapter 3

1. a. $L(u \mid \theta) = Q_1 Q_2 Q_3 P_4 P_5$

   Since we are looking at the response of one examinee on five items, we make the assumption that local independence holds. See Table 3.4.

   **TABLE 3.4**

   | $\theta$ | −1.0 | −0.9 | −0.8 | −0.7 | −0.6 | −0.5 | −0.4 | −0.3 | −0.2 | −0.1 | 0 |
   |---|---|---|---|---|---|---|---|---|---|---|---|
   | $L$ | 0.201 | 0.213 | 0.225 | 0.234 | 0.241 | 0.244 | 0.243 | 0.238 | 0.228 | 0.213 | 0.195 |

   ($L$ = Likelihood)

   b. $\hat{\theta} = -0.45$

2. a. $I(\theta) = D^2 \Sigma (a_i^2 P_i Q_i) = 5.19.$ SE$(\hat{\theta}) = 1 / \sqrt{5.19} = 0.44.$

   b. 95% confidence interval for $\theta = \hat{\theta} \pm (1.96)\text{SE} = 1.5 \pm (1.96)(0.44) = 1.5 \pm 0.86 = (0.64, 2.36)$

3. a. Since the responses of different examinees are independent, and $\theta_1, \theta_2,$ and $\theta_3$ are given, $P(U_1, U_2, U_3 \mid \theta_1, \theta_2, \theta_3) = P(U_1 \mid \theta_1)P(U_2 \mid \theta_2)P(U_3 \mid \theta_3).$ The likelihood function is, therefore,

   $$L(u_1, u_2, u_3 \mid \theta_1, \theta_2, \theta_3) = Q_1 Q_2 P_3$$
   $$= \left[ \frac{1}{1 + e^{1.7(-1-b)}} \right]\left[ \frac{1}{1 + e^{1.7(0-b)}} \right]\left[ \frac{e^{1.7(1-b)}}{1 + e^{1.7(1-b)}} \right]$$

   b. See Table 3.5.

   **TABLE 3.5**

   | $b$ | 0 | 0.1 | 0.2 | 0.3 | 0.4 | 0.5 | 0.6 | 0.7 | 0.8 | 0.9 | 1 |
   |---|---|---|---|---|---|---|---|---|---|---|---|
   | $L$ | 0.357 | 0.386 | 0.411 | 0.432 | 0.447 | 0.455 | 0.458 | 0.454 | 0.444 | 0.429 | 0.409 |

   The maximum value of the likelihood occurs at $b = 0.6$. Therefore, the maximum likelihood estimate of $b$ is 0.6.

4. a. $I(\hat{b}) = D^2 \sum_{i=1}^{N} P(\theta_i)Q(\theta_i);$ SE$(\hat{b}) = 1 / \sqrt{I(\hat{b})}$

   b. $I(\hat{b}) = 2.89 (0.062 \times 0.938 + 0.265 \times 0.735 + 0.644 \times 0.336) = 1.376;$ SE$(\hat{b}) = 0.85$

# 4

# Assessment of Model-Data Fit

Item response theory (IRT) has great potential for solving many problems in testing and measurement. The success of specific IRT applications is not assured, however, simply by processing test data through one of the computer programs described in Table 3.2. The advantages of item response models can be obtained only when the fit between the model and the test data of interest is satisfactory. A poorly fitting IRT model will not yield invariant item and ability parameters.

In many IRT applications reported in the literature, model-data fit and the consequences of misfit have not been investigated adequately. As a result, less is known about the appropriateness of particular IRT models for various applications than might be assumed from the voluminous IRT literature. In some cases goodness-of-fit studies have been conducted using what now appear to be inappropriate statistics (see, for example, Divgi, 1986; Rogers & Hattie, 1987), which may have resulted in erroneous decisions about the appropriateness of the model applied.

A further problem with many IRT goodness-of-fit studies is that too much reliance has been placed on statistical tests of model fit. These tests have a well-known and serious flaw: their sensitivity to examinee sample size. Almost any empirical departure from the model under consideration will lead to rejection of the null hypothesis of model-data fit if the sample size is sufficiently large. If sample sizes are small, even large model-data discrepancies may not be detected due to the low statistical power associated with significance tests. Moreover, parameter estimates based on small samples will be of limited usefulness because they will have large standard errors. In addition, the sampling distributions of some IRT goodness-of-fit statistics are not what they have been claimed to be; errors may be made when these statistics are interpreted in light of tabulated values of known distributions (see, for example, Divgi, 1986; Rogers & Hattie, 1987).

**TABLE 4.1** Number of Misfitting Items Detected Using the $Q_1$ Statistic

| Sample Size | Slight Misfit (2% to 3%) a = 0.9, 1.1 | Minor Misfit (4% to 5%) a = 0.8, 1.2 |
|---|---|---|
| 150 | 1 | 1 |
| 300 | 3 | 4 |
| 600 | 5 | 6 |
| 1200 | 10 | 11 |
| 2400 | 11 (22%) | 18 (36%) |

The sensitivity of goodness-of-fit statistics to sample size is illustrated in Table 4.1. A computer program, DATAGEN (Hambleton & Rovinelli, 1973), was used to simulate the item responses of 2400 examinees on a 50-item test. The items were described by two-parameter logistic ICCs, and examinee ability was simulated to have a standard normal distribution. Two simulated tests were generated: In the first, item discrimination parameters were set at either 0.90 or 1.10, with equal numbers of items at each value. This difference corresponds to a 2% or 3% difference, on the average, in the ICCs, for ability scores over the interval [−3, 3]. In the second simulated test, item discrimination parameters were set at either 0.80 or 1.20, again with equal numbers of items at each value. This difference corresponds to a 4% or 5% difference, on the average, in the ICCs, over the interval [−3, 3]. With these item discrimination values, the test data represented "slight" and "minor" departures from the assumptions of the one-parameter model. Item difficulty values were chosen to be similar to those commonly found in practice (−2.00 to +2.00).

The one-parameter model was fitted to the generated two-parameter data, and ability estimates were obtained for five overlapping samples of examinees: the first 150, the first 400, the first 600, the first 1200, and the total sample of 2400 examinees. Then, with each of the five data sets, the $Q_1$ statistic (Yen, 1981) was used to determine the number of misfitting test items at the 0.05 level of significance. The statistics in Table 4.1 clearly show the influence of sample size on detection of model-data misfit. With small samples, almost no items were detected or identified as misfitting the model; considerably more items were detected with large samples. With large sample sizes, however, even minor empirical departures from the model will result in many items being identified as misfitting, although in practice they would function quite acceptably.

Fortunately, an alternative exists to placing undue emphasis on the results of significance tests in choosing IRT models. Hambleton and Swaminathan (1985) have recommended that judgments about the fit of the model to the test data be based on three types of evidence:

1. Validity of the assumptions of the model for the test data
2. Extent to which the expected properties of the model (e.g., invariance of item and ability parameters) are obtained
3. Accuracy of model predictions using real and, if appropriate, simulated test data

Some promising goodness-of-fit analyses for amassing the three types of useful evidence have been described by Hambleton (1989) and Hambleton and Swaminathan (1985) and are summarized in Table 4.2.

Evidence of the first type, bearing on the assumptions of the model, often can be helpful in selecting IRT models for use in investigating the second and third types of evidence. Evidence of the second type, involving investigations of parameter invariance, is essential regardless of the intended application, since all IRT applications depend on this property. Evidence of the third type involves assessment of the extent to which the IRT model accounts for, or explains, the actual test results and helps in understanding the nature of model-data discrepancies and their consequences. Fitting more than one model to the test data and comparing the results to the results obtained with simulated data that were generated to fit the model of interest are especially helpful activities in choosing an appropriate model (see, for example, Hambleton & Rogers, in press).

## Checking Assumptions

Model selection can be aided by an investigation of the principal assumptions underlying the popular unidimensional item response models. Two assumptions common to all these models are that the data are unidimensional and the test administration was not speeded. An additional assumption of the two-parameter model is that guessing is minimal; a further assumption for the one-parameter model is that all item discrimination indices are equal.

**TABLE 4.2** Approaches for Assessing Goodness of Fit

*Possible Methods*

*Checking Model Assumptions*

1. Unidimensionality
   - Eigenvalue plot (from largest to smallest) of the interitem correlation matrix (tetrachoric correlations are usually preferable to phi correlations). The plot of eigenvalues is studied to determine whether a dominant first factor is present (Reckase, 1979).

   - Comparison of the plots of eigenvalues from the interitem correlation matrix using the test data, and an interitem correlation matrix of random data (the random data consist of random normal deviates in a data set with the same sample size and with the same number of variables as the test data). The two eigenvalue plots are compared. If the unidimensionality assumption is met in the test data, the two plots should be similar except for the first eigenvalue of the plot of eigenvalues for the real data. The first eigenvalue should be substantially larger than its counterpart in the random data plot (Horn, 1965). Recent modifications and examples of this method can be found in the work of Drasgow and Lissak (1983).

   - Investigation of the assumption of local independence by checking the variance-covariance or correlation matrix for examinees within different intervals on the ability or test score scale (McDonald, 1981; Tucker, Humphreys, & Roznowski, 1986). The entries in the off-diagonal elements of the matrices will be small and close to zero when the unidimensionality assumption is (approximately) met.

   - Fitting a nonlinear one-factor analysis model to the interitem correlation matrix and studying the residuals (Hattie, 1985; McDonald, 1981). Promising results from this approach were obtained by Hambleton and Rovinelli (1986).

   - Using a method of factor analysis based directly on IRT (Bock, Gibbons, & Muraki, 1988): A multidimensional version of the three-parameter normal ogive model is assumed to account for the vector of item responses. Estimation of model parameters is time-consuming and complicated but results can be obtained, and the results to date have been promising. Of special interest is the fit of a one-dimensional solution to the test data.

   - Items that appear likely to violate the assumption are checked to see whether they function differently. The *b*-values for these items are calibrated separately as a subtest and then again in the full test. The context of item calibration is unimportant if model assumptions are met. If the plot of *b*-values calibrated in the two contexts is linear with the spread comparable with the standard errors associated with the item parameter estimates, the unidimensionality assumption is viable (Bejar, 1980).

2. Equal Discrimination Indices
   - The distribution of item test score correlations (biserial or point-biserial correlations) from a standard item analysis can be reviewed. When the distribution is reasonably homogeneous, the selection of a model that assumes equal item discrimination may be viable.

**TABLE 4.2** (Continued)

---

*Possible Methods*

3. Minimal Guessing
   - The performance of low-ability students on the most difficult items can be checked. If performance levels are close to zero, the assumption is viable.

   - Plots of item-test score regressions can be helpful (Baker, 1964, 1965). Near-zero item performance for low-scoring examinees will lend support for the viability of the assumption.

   - The test difficulty, time limits, and item format should be reviewed to assess the possible role of guessing in test performance.

4. Nonspeeded (Power) Test Administration
   - The variance of number of omitted items should be compared to the variance of number of items answered incorrectly (Gulliksen, 1950). The assumption is met when the ratio is close to zero.

   - The test scores of examinees under the specified time limit and without a time limit are compared. High overlap in performance is evidence for the viability of the assumption.

   - The percentage of examinees completing the test, percentage of examinees completing 75% of the test, and the number of items completed by 80% of the examinees are reviewed. When nearly all examinees complete nearly all of the items, speed is assumed to be an unimportant factor in test performance.

*Checking Expected Model Features*

1. Invariance of Ability Parameter Estimates
   - Ability estimates are compared for different samples of test items (for example, hard and easy items; or tests reflecting different content categories within the item pool of interest). Invariance is established when the estimates do not differ in excess of the measurement errors associated with the estimates (Wright, 1968).

2. Invariance of Item Parameter Estimates
   - Comparisons of model item parameter estimates (e.g., $b$-values, $a$-values, and/or $c$-values) obtained in two or more subgroups of the population for whom the test is intended (for example, males and females; blacks, whites, and Hispanics; instructional groups; high- and low-test performers; examinees in different geographic regions). When the estimates are invariant, the plot should be linear with the amount of scatter reflecting errors due to the sample size only. Baseline plots can be obtained by using randomly equivalent samples (Shepard, Camilli, & Williams, 1984).

*Checking Model Predictions of Actual and Simulated Test Results*

   - Investigation of residuals and standardized residuals of model fit to a data set. Determination of the nature of model misfit is of value in choosing a satisfactory IRT model (see Hambleton & Swaminathan, 1985; Ludlow, 1985, 1986; Wright & Stone, 1979).

---

*(Continued)*

**TABLE 4.2** (Continued)

*Possible Methods*

- Comparisons of observed and predicted test score distributions obtained from assuming all model parameter estimates are correct. Chi-square statistics (or other statistics) or graphical methods can be used to report the results (Hambleton & Traub, 1973).

- Investigations of the effects of item placement (Kingston & Dorans, 1984; Yen, 1980), practice effects, test speededness and cheating (Drasgow, Levine, & McLaughlin, 1987), boredom (Wright & Stone, 1979), curriculum (Phillips & Mehrens, 1987), poor choice of model (Wainer & Thissen, 1987), recency of instruction (Cook, Eignor, & Taft, 1988), cognitive processing variables (Tatsuoka, 1987), and other threats to the validity of IRT results can be carried out and used to provide evidence appropriate for addressing particular IRT model uses.

- Scatterplot of ability estimates and corresponding test scores. The relationship should be strong with scatter around the test characteristic curve (reflecting measurement error) when the fit is acceptable (Lord, 1974).

- Application of a myriad of statistical tests to determine overall model fit, item fit, and person fit (see, for example, Andersen, 1973; Gustafsson, 1980b; Ludlow, 1985, 1986; Traub & Wolfe, 1981; Wright & Stone, 1979; Yen, 1981).

- Comparisons of true and estimated item and ability parameters using computer simulation methods (Hambleton & Cook, 1983).

- Investigations of model robustness using computer simulation methods. For example, the implications of fitting one-dimensional IRT models to multidimensional data can be studied (Ansley & Forsyth, 1985; Drasgow & Parsons, 1983).

Methods of studying these assumptions are summarized in Table 4.2. Regarding the assumption of unidimensionality, Hattie (1985) provided a comprehensive review of 88 indices for assessing unidimensionality and concluded that many of the methods in the older psychometric literature are unsatisfactory; methods based on nonlinear factor analysis and the analysis of residuals are the most successful. The methods described in Table 4.2 for assessing unidimensionality appear to be among the most promising at this time. Considerable research remains to be conducted on this topic, however.

The checks of other model assumptions are more straightforward. The methods in Table 4.2 use descriptive evidence provided by classical item statistics, but they still can be informative. For example, in an analysis of NAEP mathematics items (Hambleton & Swaminathan, 1985), it was learned that the item biserial correlations ranged from 0.02

to 0.97! This information indicated that it was highly unlikely that a one-parameter model would fit the test data.

## Checking Invariance

The invariance of model parameters can be assessed by means of several straightforward methods. Two of these methods are highlighted in the next section. The invariance of ability parameters can be studied by administering examinees two (or more) item sets in which the items in each set vary widely in difficulty. The item sets are constructed from the pool of test items over which ability is defined (Wright, 1968). It is common to conduct this type of study by administering both sets of test items to examinees within the same test. Ability estimates are obtained for each examinee, one from each set of items. Then the pairs of ability estimates are plotted on a graph. This plot should define a straight line with a slope of 1 because the expected ability score for each examinee does not depend on the choice of test items (provided the item response model under investigation fits the test data). Some scatter of points about the line is to be expected, however, because of measurement error. When a linear relationship with a slope of 1 and an intercept of 0 is not obtained, or the scatter exceeds that expected from knowledge of the standard errors of the ability estimates, one or more of the assumptions underlying the item response model may not hold for the data set.

## Checking Model Predictions

Several methods of checking model predictions are described in Table 4.2. One of the most promising of these methods involves the analysis of item residuals. In this method, an item response model is chosen, item and ability parameters are estimated, and predictions about the performance of various ability groups are made, assuming the validity of the chosen model. Predicted results are compared then with actual results (see, for example, Hambleton & Swaminathan, 1985; Kingston & Dorans, 1985).

A residual $r_{ij}$ (sometimes called a raw residual) is the difference between observed item performance for a subgroup of examinees and the subgroup's expected item performance:

$$r_{ij} = P_{ij} - \mathcal{E}(P_{ij})$$

where $i$ denotes the item, $j$ denotes the ability category (subgroup), $P_{ij}$ is the observed proportion of correct responses on item $i$ in the $j$th ability category, and $\mathcal{E}(P_{ij})$ is the expected proportion of correct responses obtained using the hypothesized item response model. The parameters of the hypothesized model are estimated, and the estimates are used to calculate the probability of a correct response. This probability is taken as the expected proportion correct for the ability category.

In practice, the ability continuum usually is divided into intervals of equal width (10 to 15) for the purpose of computing residuals. The intervals should be wide enough that the number of examinees in each interval is not too small, since statistics may be unstable in small samples. On the other hand, the intervals should be narrow enough that the examinees within each category are homogeneous in terms of ability.

The observed proportion correct is obtained by counting the number of examinees in an ability category who got the item right and dividing by the number of examinees in the category. To determine the expected proportion correct in an ability category, a $\theta$-value is needed. One approach is to use the midpoint of the ability category as a representative ability value for the category and to compute the probability of a correct response using this value. Alternatively, the probability of a correct response for each examinee within the ability category can be obtained, and the average of these probabilities can be used as the expected proportion.

A limitation of the raw residual is that it does not take into account the sampling error associated with the expected proportion-correct score within an ability category. To take this sampling error into account, the *standardized residual* $z_{ij}$ is computed by dividing the raw residual by the standard error of the expected proportion correct, that is,

$$z_{ij} = \frac{P_{ij} - \mathcal{E}(P_{ij})}{\sqrt{\mathcal{E}(P_{ij})\,[\,1 - \mathcal{E}(P_{ij})\,]\,/\,N_j}}$$

where $N_j$ is the number of examinees in ability category $j$.

When choosing an IRT model, a study of residuals, standardized residuals (residuals divided by their standard errors), or both, obtained for several models, can provide valuable information, as will be demonstrated in the next section.

Statistical tests, usually chi-square tests, also are applied to determine model-data fit. An extensive review of goodness-of-fit statistics is provided by Traub and Lam (1985) and Traub and Wolfe (1981). The $Q_1$ chi-square statistic (Yen, 1981) is typical of the chi-square statistics proposed by researchers for addressing model fit. The $Q_1$ statistic for item $i$ is given as

$$Q_{1i} = \sum_{j=1}^{m} \frac{N_j [P_{ij} - \mathcal{E}(P_{ij})]^2}{\mathcal{E}(P_{ij}) [1 - \mathcal{E}(P_{ij})]} \qquad [4.1]$$

$$= \sum_{j=1}^{m} z_{ij}^2$$

where examinees are divided into $m$ ability categories on the basis of their ability estimates. $P_{ij}$ and $\mathcal{E}(P_{ij})$ were defined earlier. The statistic $Q_1$ is distributed as a chi-square with degrees of freedom equal to $m - k$, where $k$ is the number of parameters in the IRT model. If the observed value of the statistic exceeds the critical value (obtained from the chi-square table), the null hypothesis that the ICC fits the data is rejected and a better fitting model must be found.

## Examples of Goodness-of-Fit Analyses

The purpose of this section is to provide an example of procedures for investigating model-data fit using 75 items from the 1982 version of the New Mexico High School Proficiency Test. The items on this test are multiple-choice items with four choices, and we had access to the item responses of 2000 examinees. Normally, the first steps in the investigation would be as follows:

1. Conduct a classical item analysis.
2. Determine the dominance of the first factor, and check other IRT model assumptions.
3. Make a preliminary selection of promising IRT models.
4. Obtain item and ability parameter estimates for the models of interest.

The results of the item analysis are reported in the Appendix A. If we had found substantial variation in the item point-biserial correlations, our interest in the one-parameter model would have been low. If all of the items were relatively easy, or if the test had consisted of short free-response items, we probably would not have worked with the three-parameter model, at least at the outset. The item analysis reveals that the variation in item difficulties and discrimination indices is substantial and, therefore, the one-parameter model may not be appropriate. Nevertheless, for illustrative purposes, we will fit the one-, two-, and three-parameter models and compare the results. In general, comparisons of the fits of different models will facilitate the choice of an appropriate model.

Figure 4.1 clearly shows the dominance of the first factor. The largest eigenvalue of the correlation matrix for the 75 items is over five times larger than the second largest, and the second largest eigenvalue is hardly distinguishable from the smaller ones. Had the plot of eigenvalues produced a less conclusive result, the method of Drasgow and Lissak (1983) should have been used. In this method the plot of eigenvalues resulting from a correlation matrix derived from (uncorrelated) normal deviates is obtained and is used to provide an indication of the eigenvalues that result from chance factors alone. This plot serves as a baseline for interpreting eigenvalues and (ultimately) the dimensionality of the real data.

Appendix A contains the item parameter estimates obtained from fitting one-, two-, and three-parameter logistic models. These statistics were obtained by using LOGIST and scaling the ability scores to a mean of 0 and a standard deviation of 1.

The next activity was to investigate the invariance of the item parameters for the three-parameter model. (Similar analyses were carried out with the one- and two-parameter models but are not reported here.) The sample of 2000 examinees was split into two randomly equivalent groups of 1000. In a second split, two ability groups were formed: the top half of the distribution and the bottom half of the distribution. A total of four groups of 1000 was available for subsequent analyses. Through use of the ability scores obtained from the total-group analysis, four three-parameter-model LOGIST analyses were conducted, one with each group, to obtain item parameter estimates. Figure 2.6 provides the baseline information for the $b$ parameter. This figure provides an indication of the variability that could be expected in the item parameter estimates due to the use of randomly equivalent groups of

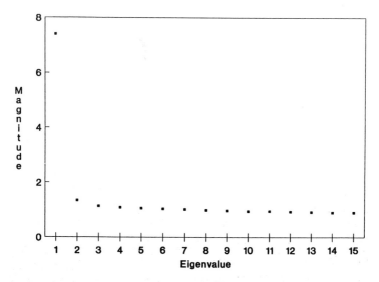

**Figure 4.1.** Plot of the Largest 15 Eigenvalues

size $n = 1000$, that is, due to sampling error. If item difficulty parameter invariance has been obtained, a scatterplot similar to that shown in Figure 2.6 should be obtained from the high-and-low-performing groups of examinees. In fact, Figures 2.6 and 4.2 are quite similar, indicating that item parameter invariance is present. What also is revealed in Figure 4.2 is that item parameters for easy items are not well estimated in the high-performing group or the hard items in the low-performing group, as demonstrated by the "dumbbell" shaped scatterplots. The implications for parameter estimation are clear: Heterogeneous samples of examinees are needed to obtain stable item parameter estimates (see, for example, Stocking, 1990).

Invariance of ability parameters across different samples of items was investigated next. Invariance of ability parameters over randomly equivalent forms (e.g., ability estimates based on examinee performance on the odd-numbered items and on the even-numbered items) indicates the variability due to the sampling of test items. A more rigorous test of invariance would be a comparison of ability estimates over (say) tests consisting of the easiest and hardest items in the item bank.

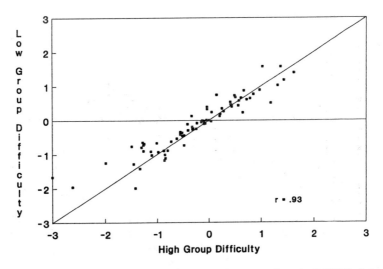

**Figure 4.2.** Plot of 3P Item Difficulty Values Based on Samples of Differing Ability

Figures 4.3 and 4.4 provide comparisons between ability estimates obtained with the randomly equivalent subtests and the hard versus easy subtests for the three-parameter model. Item parameter estimates used in the calculation of ability scores were obtained from the total sample ($N$ = 2000) and are reported in the Appendix. These comparisons provide evidence of the invariance of ability parameters over tests of varying difficulty (note that the two plots are similar and scattered about the line with slope 1). These plots also show the generally large errors in ability estimation for low- and high-ability examinees (Figure 4.3) and even larger errors in ability estimation for low-ability examinees on hard tests and for high-ability examinees on easy tests (Figure 4.4). These findings may have more to say about improper test design than parameter invariance, however.

Based on the plots, it appears that item and ability parameter invariance was obtained with the three-parameter model. The plots also indicate that satisfactory ability estimation requires that examinees be administered test items that are matched with their ability levels and that satisfactory item parameter estimation requires heterogeneous ability distributions.

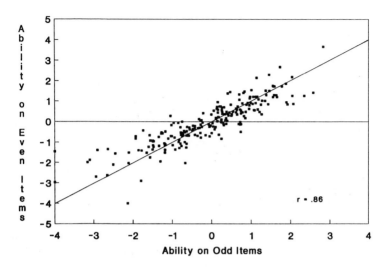

**Figure 4.3.** Plot of 3P Ability Estimates Based on Equivalent Test Halves (Odd vs. Even Items)

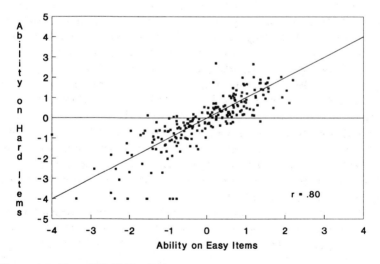

**Figure 4.4.** Plot of 3P Ability Estimates Based on Tests of Differing Difficulty (Hardest vs. Easiest Items)

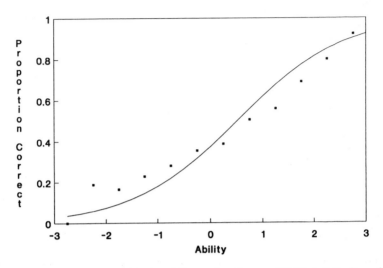

**Figure 4.5.** Observed and Expected Proportion Correct (1P Model) for Item 6

Perhaps the most valuable goodness-of-fit data of all are provided by residuals (and/or standardized residuals). Normally, these are best interpreted with the aid of graphs. Figures 4.5 to 4.7 provide the residuals (computed in 12 equally spaced ability categories between −3.0 and +3.0) obtained with the one-, two-, and three-parameter models, respectively, for Item 6. The best fitting ICCs using the item parameter estimates given in the Appendix also appear in the figures. When the residuals are small and randomly distributed about the ICC, we can conclude that the ICC fits the item performance data. Figure 4.5 clearly shows that the one-parameter model does not match examinee performance data at the low and high ends of the ability scale. The fit is improved with the two-parameter model (Figure 4.6) because the discrimination parameter adjusts the slope of the ICC. The fit is further improved with the three-parameter model (Figure 4.7) because the $c$ parameter takes into account the performance of the low-ability examinees.

An analysis of residuals, as reflected in Figures 4.5 to 4.7, is helpful in judging model-data fit. Figures 4.8 to 4.10 show the plots of standardized residuals against ability levels obtained with the one-, two-, and three-parameter models, respectively, for Item 6. The observed pattern of standardized residuals shown in Figure 4.8 is due to the fact

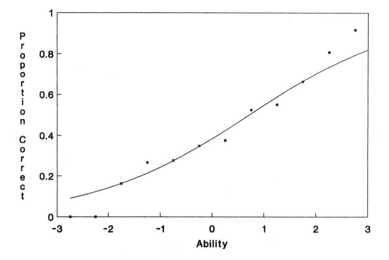

**Figure 4.6.** Observed and Expected Proportion Correct (2P Model) for Item 6

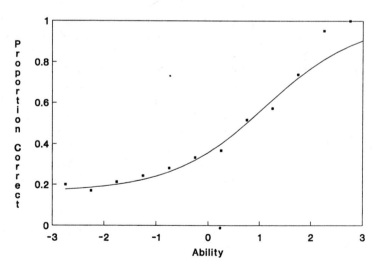

**Figure 4.7.** Observed and Expected Proportion Correct (3P Model) for Item 6

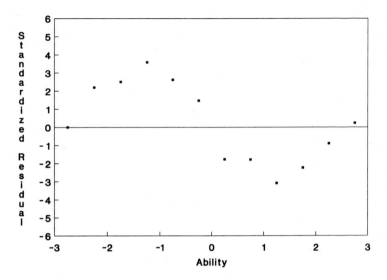

**Figure 4.8.** 1P Standardized Residuals for Item 6

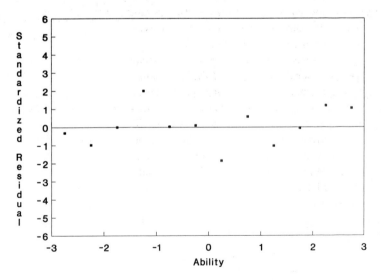

**Figure 4.9.** 2P Standardized Residuals for Item 6

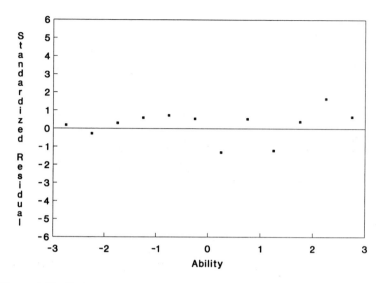

**Figure 4.10.** 3P Standardized Residuals for Item 6

that the item is less discriminating than the average level of discrimination adopted for all items in the one-parameter model. Clear improvements are gained by using the two-parameter model. The gains from using the three-parameter over the two-parameter model are much smaller but noticeable.

Item 6 was selected for emphasis because of its pedagogical value, but in general the two- and three-parameter models fit data for the 75 test items better than the one-parameter model.

With 12 ability categories and a 75-item test, 900 standardized residuals were available for analysis. The expected distribution of standardized residuals under the null hypothesis that the model fits the test data is unknown, although one might expect the distribution of standardized residuals to be (approximately) normal with mean 0 and standard deviation 1. Rather than make the assumption of a normal distribution, however, it is possible to use computer simulation methods to generate a distribution of standardized residuals under the null hypothesis that the model fits the data, and use this distribution as a basis for interpreting the actual distribution.

To generate the distribution of standardized residuals for the one-parameter model when the model fits the test data, item and ability

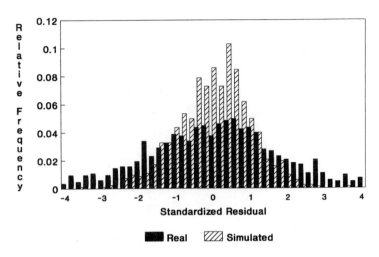

**Figure 4.11.** Frequency Distributions of Standardized Residuals for 1P Real and Simulated Data

parameter estimates for the model (reported in the Appendix) are assumed to be true. Item response data then can be generated (Hambleton & Rovinelli, 1973) using these parameter values, and a one-parameter model fitted to the data. Standardized residuals are obtained, and the distribution of standardized residuals is formed. This distribution serves as the empirically generated "sampling distribution" of standardized residuals under the null hypothesis that the model fits the data. This distribution serves as the baseline for interpreting the distribution of standardized residuals obtained with the real test data.

In Figure 4.11, the real and simulated distributions of standardized residuals for the one-parameter model are very different. The simulated data were distributed normally; the real data were distributed more uniformly. Clearly, since the distributions are very different, the one-parameter model does not fit the data.

Figures 4.12 and 4.13 show the real and simulated distributions of standardized residuals obtained with the two- and three-parameter models, respectively. The evidence is clear that substantial improvements in fit are obtained with the more general models, with the three-parameter model fitting the data very well. The real and simulated distributions for the three-parameter model are nearly identical.

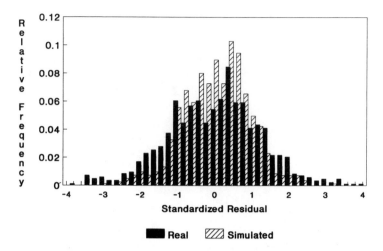

**Figure 4.12.** Frequency Distributions of Standardized Residuals for 2P Real and Simulated Data

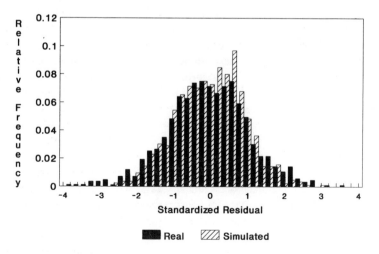

**Figure 4.13.** Frequency Distributions of Standardized Residuals for 3P Real and Simulated Data

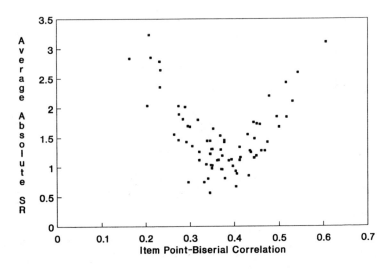

**Figure 4.14.** Plot of 1P Average Absolute Standardized Residuals Against Point-Biserial Correlations

Other types of goodness-of-fit evidence also can be obtained. Figures 4.14, 4.15, and 4.16 show the relationship between item misfit statistics and item point-biserial correlations for the one-, two-, and three-parameter models, respectively. In this analysis, item misfit was determined by averaging the absolute values of standardized residuals obtained after fitting the model of interest to the item data.

Figure 4.14 shows the inadequacy of the one-parameter model in fitting items with high or low discrimination indices. Figure 4.15 shows that the pattern of item misfit changes substantially with the two-parameter model. Figure 4.16, for the three-parameter model, is similar to Figure 4.15 except the sizes of the item misfit statistics are generally a bit smaller.

The complete set of analyses described here (and others that were not described because of space limitations) are helpful in choosing an IRT model. For these test data, evidence was found that the test was uni-dimensional and that the fit of the three-parameter model was very good and substantially better than that of the one-parameter model and somewhat better than that of the two-parameter model. Many of the baseline results were especially helpful in judging model-data fit.

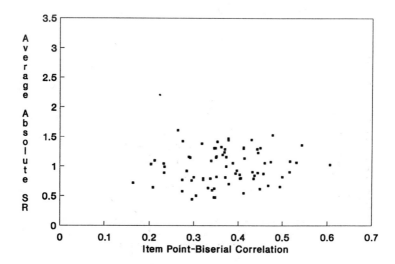

**Figure 4.15.**  Plot of 2P Average Absolute Standardized Residuals Against Point-Biserial Correlations

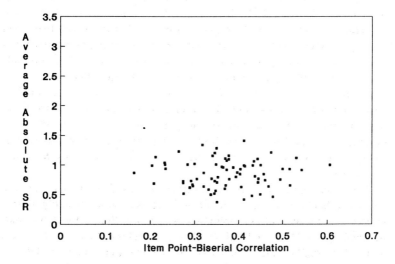

**Figure 4.16.**  Plot of 3P Average Absolute Standardized Residuals Against Point-Biserial Correlations

## Summary

In assessing model-data fit, the best approach involves (a) designing and conducting a variety of analyses designed to detect expected types of misfit, (b) considering the full set of results carefully, and (c) making a judgment about the suitability of the model for the intended application. Analyses should include investigations of model assumptions, of the extent to which desired model features are obtained, and of differences between model predictions and actual data. Statistical tests may be carried out, but care must be taken in interpreting the statistical information. The number of investigations that may be conducted is almost limitless. The amount of effort and money expended in collecting, analyzing, and interpreting results should be consistent with the importance and nature of the intended application.

## Exercises for Chapter 4

1. Suppose that a three-parameter model was fitted to a set of test data. The item parameter estimates for a particular item were $a = 1.23$; $b = 0.76$; $c = 0.25$. In order to assess the fit of the model to this item, the examinees were divided into five ability groups on the basis of their ability estimates, with 20 examinees in each group. The item responses for the examinees in each ability group are given in Table 4.3.

**TABLE 4.3**

| θ Level | Item Responses | | | | | | | | | | | | | | | | | | | |
|---------|---|---|---|---|---|---|---|---|---|---|---|---|---|---|---|---|---|---|---|---|
| -2.0 | 0 | 0 | 0 | 0 | 1 | 0 | 0 | 0 | 0 | 0 | 1 | 0 | 0 | 0 | 0 | 0 | 0 | 1 | 0 | 1 |
| -1.0 | 0 | 1 | 0 | 1 | 0 | 0 | 1 | 0 | 0 | 0 | 0 | 1 | 0 | 0 | 0 | 1 | 0 | 0 | 0 | 0 |
| 0.0 | 1 | 0 | 0 | 0 | 1 | 1 | 0 | 0 | 0 | 0 | 1 | 0 | 0 | 1 | 0 | 0 | 1 | 0 | 1 | 1 |
| 1.0 | 1 | 1 | 1 | 1 | 1 | 1 | 1 | 0 | 1 | 1 | 1 | 0 | 1 | 1 | 0 | 1 | 0 | 1 | 0 | 1 |
| 2.0 | 1 | 1 | 1 | 1 | 1 | 1 | 1 | 1 | 1 | 1 | 0 | 1 | 1 | 1 | 1 | 1 | 1 | 0 | 1 | 1 |

a. Calculate the observed proportion correct at each ability level.

b. Calculate the expected proportion correct at each ability level (using the parameter estimates given).

c. Calculate the $Q_1$ goodness-of-fit statistic for this item. What are the degrees of freedom for the chi-square test?

d. Does the three-parameter model appear to fit the data for this item?

2. Suppose that one- and two-parameter models also were fitted to the data. The item parameter estimates for the two models are given below:

$$\text{One-parameter model:} \quad b = 0.17$$
$$\text{Two-parameter model:} \quad b = 0.18; \quad a = 0.56$$

a. Calculate the $Q_1$ statistics for assessing the fit of the one- and two-parameter models (assume that the ability intervals are the same).

b. Does the one- or two-parameter model appear to fit the data?

c. Based on your results, which IRT model appears to be most appropriate for the data given?

## Answers to Exercises for Chapter 4

1. a. $\theta = -2$: $p = 0.20$; $\theta = -1$: $p = 0.25$; $\theta = 0$: $p = 0.40$; $\theta = 1$: $p = 0.75$; $\theta = 2$: $p = 0.90$.

   b. $P(\theta = -2) = 0.25$; $P(\theta = -1) = 0.27$; $P(\theta = 0) = 0.38$; $P(\theta = 1) = 0.72$; $P(\theta = 2) = 0.95$.

   c. $$Q_1 = \sum_{j=1}^{m} \frac{N_j\,[P_j - \mathcal{E}(P_j)\,]^2}{\mathcal{E}(P_j)\,[1 - \mathcal{E}(P_j)\,]}$$

   $$= \frac{20\,(0.20 - 0.25)^2}{0.25 \times 0.75} + \frac{20\,(0.25 - 0.27)^2}{0.27 \times 0.73} + \frac{20\,(0.40 - 0.38)^2}{0.38 \times 0.62}$$

   $$+ \frac{20\,(0.75 - 0.72)^2}{0.72 \times 0.28} + \frac{20\,(0.90 - 0.95)^2}{0.95 \times 0.05}$$

   $$= 1.48$$

   degrees of freedom = $5 - 3 = 2$

   d. $\chi^2_{2,.05} = 5.99$. Since the calculated value does not exceed the tabulated value, we can conclude that the three-parameter model fits the data for this item.

2. a. $$Q_1 = \sum_{j=1}^{m} \frac{N_j\,[P_j - \mathcal{E}(P_j)\,]^2}{\mathcal{E}(P_j)\,[1 - \mathcal{E}(P_j)\,]}$$

For the one-parameter model,

$$Q_1 = \frac{20\,(0.20 - 0.02)^2}{0.02 \times 0.98} + \frac{20\,(0.25 - 0.12)^2}{0.12 \times 0.88} + \frac{20\,(0.40 - 0.43)^2}{0.43 \times 0.57}$$

$$+ \frac{20\,(0.75 - 0.80)^2}{0.80 \times 0.20} + \frac{20\,(0.90 - 0.96)^2}{0.96 \times 0.04}$$

$$= 38.52$$

For the two-parameter model,

$$Q_1 = \frac{20\,(0.20 - 0.11)^2}{0.11 \times 0.89} + \frac{20\,(0.25 - 0.25)^2}{0.25 \times 0.75} + \frac{20\,(0.40 - 0.46)^2}{0.46 \times 0.54}$$

$$+ \frac{20\,(0.75 - 0.69)^2}{0.69 \times 0.31} + \frac{20\,(0.90 - 0.85)^2}{0.85 \times 0.15}$$

$$= 2.67$$

b. The one-parameter model does not fit the data, but the two-parameter model does.

c. While the three-parameter model fits the data better than the two-parameter model, the two-parameter model fits the data almost as well. In the interests of parsimony, the model of choice would be the two-parameter model.

# 5

# The Ability Scale

The ultimate purpose of testing is to assign a "score" to an examinee that reflects the examinee's level of attainment of a skill (or level of acquisition of an attribute) as measured by the test. Needless to say, the assigned score must be interpreted with care and must be valid for its intended use (Linn, 1990).

In typical achievement measurement, the examinee is assigned a score on the basis of his or her responses to a set of dichotomously scored items. In the classical test theory framework, the assigned score is the number of correct responses. This number-right score is an unbiased estimate of the examinee's true score on the test. In item response theory it is assumed that an examinee has an underlying "ability" $\theta$ that determines his or her probability of giving a correct response to an item. Again, based on the responses of the examinee to a set of items, an ability score $\theta$ is assigned to an examinee. Unfortunately, $\theta$ is not as easily determined as the number-right score. Through use of the methods described in chapter 3, an estimate of ability $\theta$ is obtained for an examinee. As we shall see later, the ability $\theta$ of an examinee is monotonically related to the examinee's true score (assuming that the item response model fits the data); that is, the relationship between $\theta$ and the true score is nonlinear and strictly increasing.

The general scheme for determining an examinee's ability is as follows:

1. An examinee's responses to a set of items are obtained and coded as 1 (for correct answers) or 0 (for incorrect answers).
2. When the item parameters that characterize an item are assumed to be known (as happens when item parameters are available for a bank of items), the ability $\theta$ is estimated using one of the methods indicated in chapter 3.

3. When the item parameters that characterize the items are not known, the item and ability parameters must be estimated from the same response data, and one of the procedures described in chapter 3 must be employed.

4. The estimated ability value is reported as is, or is transformed using a linear or a nonlinear transformation to a more convenient scale (e.g., without negatives or decimals) to aid in the interpretation of the score. The SAT and NAEP reporting scales are well-known examples of scales obtained by transforming original score scales.

At all stages of analysis and interpretation, the issue of the validity of the ability score must be considered (Linn, 1990). Every attempt must be made to validate the ability score. The validity information available for the number-right score or any transformation of it may not be relevant or appropriate for the ability score and, hence, a validity study specifically designed for the ability score may be needed. Refer to Hambleton and Swaminathan (1985, chapter 4) for more details on this important issue.

What is the nature of the ability score? On what scale is it measured? What transformations are meaningful? These important issues are discussed next.

### The Nature of the Ability Scale

As mentioned above, the number-right score, denoted as $X$, is an unbiased estimate of the true score, $\tau$. By definition,

$$\mathcal{E}(X) = \tau$$

The number-right score, $X$, may be divided by the number of items (i.e., linearly transformed) to yield a proportion-correct score. The proportion-correct score is meaningful and appropriate when the test is subdivided into subtests, each with different numbers of items, measuring (say) a number of different objectives. This is usually the practice with criterion-referenced tests. When the test is norm-referenced, other linear transformations may be used to yield standard scores. In addition, when it is necessary to compare examinees, the score $X$ may be transformed nonlinearly to yield stanines, percentiles, and so on.

While the above transformations greatly facilitate the interpretation of the score $X$, its major drawback remains. The score $X$ is not independent of the items to which the examinee responds, and the transformed scores are not independent of the group of examinees to which they are referenced. The ability score θ, on the other hand, possesses such independence. As described previously, θ is independent of the particular set of items administered to the examinees, and the population to which the examinee belongs. This invariance property is what distinguishes the θ score from the score $X$. Since it is possible to compare examinees who respond to different sets of items when using the θ score, the θ scale may be thought of as an absolute scale with respect to the trait or ability that is being measured.

It is important, at this point, to discuss the nature or meaning of the term *ability* or *trait*. Clearly, these are labels that describe what the set of test items measures. An ability or trait may be defined broadly as aptitude or achievement, a narrowly defined achievement variable (e.g., ability to add three two-digit integers), or a personality variable (e.g., self-concept, motivation). An ability or trait is not necessarily something innate or immutable. In fact, the term *ability* or *trait* may be improper or misleading to the extent that it connotes a fixed characteristic of the examinee; the term *proficiency level,* for example, may be more appropriate in many instances.

What is the nature of the scale on which θ is defined? Clearly, the observed score $X$ is not defined on a ratio scale. In fact, $X$ may not even be defined on an interval scale. At best, we may treat $X$ as being defined on an ordinal scale. The same applies to the scale on which θ is defined. In some instances, however, a "limited" ratio-scale interpretation of the θ-scale may be possible.

## Transformation of the θ-Scale

In item response models, the probability of a correct response is given by the item response function, $P(\theta)$. If, in Equations 2.2 or 2.3, θ is replaced by $\theta^* = \alpha\theta + \beta$, $b$ by $b^* = \alpha b + \beta$, and $a$ by $a^* = a/\alpha$, then

$$P(\theta^*) = P(\theta)$$

Thus, θ, $b$, and $a$ may be transformed linearly without altering the probability of a correct response (the implications of this "indeterminacy" will be discussed further in later chapters), meaning that the $\theta$-scale may be transformed linearly as long as the item parameter values also are transformed appropriately.

Recall that $\theta$ is defined in the interval $(-\infty, \infty)$. Woodcock (1978), in defining the scale for the Woodcock–Johnson Psycho–Educational Battery, employed the one-parameter model and the scale

$$w_\theta = 20 \log_9(e^\theta) + 500$$

that is, used a logarithmic scale to the base 9. Since

$$\log_9(e^\theta) = \theta \log_9 e$$

and

$$\log_9 e = 0.455$$

then

$$w_\theta = 9.1\theta + 500$$

Thus, the Woodcock–Johnson scale is a linear scale. The item difficulties were transformed in the same manner,

$$w_b = 9.1b + 500$$

The $w_\theta$ scale has the property that the differences $(w_\theta - w_b) = 20, 10, 0, -10, -20$ correspond to the probabilities of correct responses of 0.90, 0.75, 0.50, 0.25, and 0.10, respectively. Wright (1977) modified this scale as

$$w = 9.1\theta + 100$$

and termed it the WITs scale.

The transformations of the $\theta$-scale described above are *linear*. Nonlinear transformations of the $\theta$-scale may be more useful in some cases. Consider the nonlinear transformation

$$\theta^* = e^{D\theta}$$

and the corresponding transformation of the difficulty parameter

$$b^* = e^{Db}$$

Then, for the one-parameter model

$$P(\theta) = \frac{e^{D(\theta - b)}}{1 + e^{D(\theta - b)}}$$

$$= \frac{e^{D\theta}}{e^{Db} + e^{D\theta}}$$

$$= \frac{\theta^*}{b^* + \theta^*}$$

Hence,

$$P(\theta^*) = \frac{\theta^*}{b^* + \theta^*}$$

It is of interest to note that Rasch first developed the one-parameter model using the form given above for the probability of success.

The probability of an incorrect response on the $\theta^*$ scale, $Q(\theta^*) = 1 - P(\theta^*)$, is

$$Q(\theta^*) = \frac{b^*}{\theta^* + b^*}$$

The odds $O$ for success, defined as $P(\theta^*) / Q(\theta^*)$, are then

$$O = \frac{\theta^*}{b^*}$$

Consider two examinees with ability $\theta_1^*$ and $\theta_2^*$ responding to an item, and denote their odds for success as $O_1$ and $O_2$. Then

$$O_1 = \frac{\theta_1^*}{b^*} \qquad \text{and} \qquad O_2 = \frac{\theta_2^*}{b^*}$$

The ratio of their odds for success is

$$\frac{O_1}{O_2} = \frac{\theta_1^*}{\theta_2^*}$$

Thus, an examinee with twice the ability of another examinee, measured on the $\theta^*$-scale, has twice the odds of successfully answering the item. In this sense, the $\theta^*$-scale has the properties of a ratio scale. The same property also holds for the item; for an examinee responding to two items with difficulty values $b_1^*$ and $b_2^*$ (measured on the $b^*$-scale), the odds for success are $O_1 = \theta^* / b_1^*$ and $O_2 = \theta^* / b_2^*$. The ratio of the odds for the examinee is

$$\frac{O_1}{O_2} = \frac{b_2^*}{b_1^*}$$

If $b_2^* = 2b_1^*$ (i.e., the first item is twice as easy as the second item), the odds for successfully answering the easy item are twice those for successfully answering the harder item.

The ratio-scale property for $\theta^*$- and $b^*$-scales, as defined above, holds only for the one-parameter model. For the two- and three-parameter models the scale must be defined differently (see Hambleton & Swaminathan, 1985).

Another nonlinear transformation that is meaningful for the one-parameter model is the "log-odds" transformation. Since, for two examinees responding to the same item

$$\frac{O_1}{O_2} = \frac{O_1^*}{O_2^*} = \frac{e^{D\theta_1}}{e^{D\theta_2}} = e^{D(\theta_1 - \theta_2)},$$

$$\ln \frac{O_1}{O_2} = D(\theta_1 - \theta_2)$$

where ln is the natural logarithm (to the base e). Typically, in the one-parameter model, $D$ is omitted so that

$$P(\theta) = \frac{e^{(\theta - b)}}{[1 + e^{(\theta - b)}]}$$

Omitting $D$ in "log-odds" expressions, we have

$$\ln \frac{O_1}{O_2} = \theta_1 - \theta_2$$

If abilities differ by one point,

$$\ln \frac{O_1}{O_2} = 1$$

then

$$\frac{O_1}{O_2} = e^1 = 2.718$$

Thus, a difference of one point on the ability scale corresponds to a factor of 2.72 in odds for success on the $\theta$-scale. Similarly, if an examinee responds to two items with difficulty values $b_1$ and $b_2$,

$$\ln \frac{O_1}{O_2} = b_2 - b_1$$

As before, a difference of one unit in item difficulties corresponds to a factor of 2.72 in the odds for success.

The units on the log-odds scale are called *logits*. The logit units can be obtained directly as follows: Since

$$P(\theta) = \frac{e^{(\theta - b)}}{1 + e^{(\theta - b)}} \quad \text{and} \quad Q(\theta) = \frac{1}{1 + e^{(\theta - b)}}$$

thus

$$\frac{P(\theta)}{Q(\theta)} = e^{(\theta - b)}$$

Hence

$$\ln \frac{P(\theta)}{Q(\theta)} = \theta - b$$

## Transformation to the True-Score Scale

The most important transformation of the $\theta$-scale is to the true-score scale. Let $X$, the number-right score, be defined as

$$X = \sum_{j=1}^{n} U_j$$

where $U_j$ is the 1 or 0 response of an examinee to item $j$. If we denote the true score by $\tau$, then

$$\tau = \mathcal{E}(X) = \mathcal{E}\left(\sum_{j=1}^{n} U_j\right)$$

By the linear nature of the expectation operator,

$$\mathcal{E}\left(\sum_{j=1}^{n} U_j\right) = \sum_{j=1}^{n} \mathcal{E}(U_j)$$

Now, if a random variable $Y$ takes on values $y_1$ and $y_2$ with probabilities $P_1$ and $P_2$, then

$$\mathcal{E}(Y) = y_1 P_1 + y_2 P_2$$

Since $U_j$ takes on value 1 with probability $P_j(\theta)$ and value 0 with probability $Q_j(\theta) = 1 - P_j(\theta)$, it follows that

$$\mathcal{E}(U_j) = 1 \cdot P_j(\theta) + 0 \cdot Q_j(\theta) = P_j(\theta)$$

Thus,

$$\tau = \sum_{j=1}^{n} P_j(\theta)$$

that is, the true score of an examinee with ability $\theta$ is the sum of the item characteristic curves. The true score, $\tau$ in this case, is called the *test characteristic curve* because it is the sum of the item characteristic curves. In the strict sense, the above relationship holds only when the item response model fits the data. To emphasize this, the true score $\tau$ is indicated as $\tau \mid \theta$, that is,

$$\tau \mid \theta = \sum_{j=1}^{n} P_j(\theta).$$

When no ambiguity exists, the notation $\tau \mid \theta$ will be shortened to $\tau$.

The true score $\tau$ and $\theta$ are monotonically related; that is, the true score may be considered to be a nonlinear transformation of $\theta$. Since $P_j(\theta)$ is between 0 and 1, $\tau$ is between 0 and $n$. Hence, $\tau$ is on the same scale as the number-right score, except that $\tau$ can assume non-integer as well as integer values. The transformation from $\theta$ to $\tau$ is useful in reporting ability values; instead of the $\theta$ values, $\tau$ values that lie in the range 0 to $n$ are reported. Alternatively, $\pi$, the true proportion correct or domain score, obtained by dividing $\tau$ by the number of items $n$, can be reported. In this case,

$$\pi = \frac{1}{n} \sum_{j=1}^{n} P_j(\theta)$$

While $-\infty < \theta < \infty$, $\pi$ lies between 0 and 1 (or, in terms of percentages, between 0% and 100%).

The lower limit for $\pi$ for the one- and two-parameter models is zero. For the three-parameter model, however, as $\theta$ approaches $-\infty$, $P_j(\theta)$ approaches $c_j$, the lower asymptote. Thus, the lower limit for $\pi$ is $\Sigma c_j / n$. Correspondingly, the lower limit for $\tau$ is $\Sigma c_j$.

The transformation of $\theta$ to the true score or the domain score has important implications. First, and most obvious, is that negative scores are eliminated. Second, the transformation yields a scale that ranges from 0 to $n$ (or 0% to 100% if the domain score is used), which is readily interpretable. When pass-fail decisions must be made, it is often difficult to set a cut-off score on the $\theta$-scale. Since the domain-score scale is familiar, a cut-off score (such as 80% mastery) is typically set on the domain-score scale. The domain score is plotted against $\theta$, and the $\theta$ value corresponding to the domain score value is identified as the

**TABLE 5.1** Item Parameters for Five Test Items

| Item | $b_i$ | Parameters $a_i$ | $c_i$ |
|------|-------|------------------|-------|
| 1 | −2.00 | 0.80 | 0.00 |
| 2 | −1.00 | 1.00 | 0.00 |
| 3 | 0.00 | 1.20 | 0.10 |
| 4 | 1.00 | 1.50 | 0.15 |
| 5 | 2.00 | 2.00 | 0.20 |

cut-off score on the θ-scale (see, for example, Hambleton & de Gruitjer, 1983). Alternatively, all θ values can be converted to domain-score values and the pass–fail decision made with respect to the domain-score scale.

To illustrate the conversion of θ values to domain-score values, we shall consider a test with five items. The item parameter values for these items are given in Table 5.1.

For each item,

1. The probability of a correct response is computed at θ = −3, −2, −1, 0, 1, 2, 3 using the three-parameter model (Equation 2.3).
2. These probabilities are summed over the five items at each of the θ values to yield

$$\sum_{j=1}^{5} P_j(\theta)$$

3. The domain score π is obtained at each θ value by dividing the sum in the equation above by 5.
4. The resulting relationship between π and θ at the θ values is tabulated.

We now have the functional relationship between π and θ at θ = −3, −2, −1, 0, 1, 2, 3. This is a monotonically increasing relationship and can be plotted as a graph. The computations are given in Table 5.2.

The final implication of the θ to τ (or θ to π) conversion is that the true score τ (or π) of an examinee whose ability value is known (or estimated) can be computed on a set of items not administered to the examinee! When the item parameters for a set of items are given, an

**TABLE 5.2** Relationship Between $\theta$ and $\pi$

| $\theta$ | $P_1(\theta)$ | $P_2(\theta)$ | $P_3(\theta)$ | $P_4(\theta)$ | $P_5(\theta)$ | $\tau = \Sigma P_i(\theta)$ | $\pi = \tau/n$ |
|---|---|---|---|---|---|---|---|
| -3 | 0.20 | 0.03 | 0.10 | 0.15 | 0.20 | 0.69 | 0.14 |
| -2 | 0.50 | 0.15 | 0.11 | 0.15 | 0.20 | 1.12 | 0.22 |
| -1 | 0.80 | 0.50 | 0.20 | 0.16 | 0.20 | 1.85 | 0.37 |
| 0 | 0.94 | 0.85 | 0.55 | 0.21 | 0.20 | 2.75 | 0.55 |
| 1 | 0.98 | 0.97 | 0.90 | 0.58 | 0.22 | 3.65 | 0.73 |
| 2 | 0.99 | 0.99 | 0.99 | 0.94 | 0.60 | 4.51 | 0.90 |
| 3 | 1.00 | 1.00 | 1.00 | 1.00 | 0.96 | 4.96 | 0.99 |

examinee's true score can be computed as long as his or her $\theta$ value is known, as indicated in the illustration, allowing the projection or prediction of an examinee's true score or pass-fail status on a new set of items. This feature is used in "customized testing" (Linn & Hambleton, 1990). The fact that an examinee's true score can be computed on any set of items also is used in the procedure for determining the scaling constants for placing the item parameters of two tests on a common scale (see chapter 9 on equating).

## Summary

The ability $\theta$ of an examinee, together with the item parameter values, determines the examinee's probability of responding correctly to an item. Based on the examinee's response to a set of items, an ability score may be assigned to the examinee. The most important feature of the $\theta$ score that distinguishes it from the number-right score is that $\theta$ does not depend on the particular set of items administered to the examinee. Examinees who are administered different sets of items can be compared with respect to their $\theta$ values. In this sense, the $\theta$-scale may be considered an absolute scale.

The $\theta$ values may be transformed linearly to facilitate interpretation. The $\theta$-scale, or any linear transformation of it, however, does not possess the properties of ratio or interval scales, although it is popular and reasonable to assume that the $\theta$-scale has equal-interval scale properties. In some instances, however, a nonlinear transformation of the $\theta$-scale may provide a ratio-scale type of interpretation. The transformation $\theta^* = e^\theta$ and $b^* = e^b$ for the one-parameter model provides a ratio-scale interpretation for the odds for success. The "log-odds" transformation also enables such interpretations. For the two- and three-parameter models such simple transformations are not available.

The most important nonlinear transformation of the $\theta$-scale is the transformation that yields the true-score scale. When the item response model fits the data, the true score is the sum of the item characteristic curves evaluated at a specified value of $\theta$. Because it is the sum of item characteristic curves, the ability to true-score conversion is also known as the test characteristic curve. The true score is on the same metric as the number-right score. If desired, the true score may be converted to the domain score (or proportion-correct score) by dividing the true score by the number of items. The true score or the proportion-correct score has intuitive appeal and, hence, is often employed to set cut-off scores for making mastery-nonmastery decisions. The true score or the domain score can be computed for any set of items (including those not taken by the examinee) as long as the examinee's ability and the item parameters are known. Such "predictions" of an examinee's true score on a set of "new" items may provide valuable information regarding the use or inclusion of these items in a test.

## Exercises for Chapter 5

1. Suppose that ability estimates for a group of examinees on a test are in the range $(-4, 4)$.
   a. What linear transformation is appropriate to produce a scale on which the scores are positive integers (assuming that $\hat{\theta}$ is obtained to two decimal places)?
   b. What nonlinear transformation is appropriate for producing scores that range from 0 to 100?
2. In Table 5.2, the relationship between $\theta$ and $\pi$ is tabulated.
   a. Plot a graph of $\pi$ (on the $y$-axis) against $\theta$ (on the $x$-axis). What can you say about the shape of the curve?
   b. Suppose that only students who have answered at least 80% of the items correctly are considered "masters"; that is, the cut-off score is set at $\pi = 0.80$. If an examinee has an ability score of 1.2, may this examinee be considered a master?
   c. What is the $\theta$ value that corresponds to a cut-off score of $\pi = 0.80$?

3. An examinee has an ability score of $\theta = 1.5$ as determined by his or her performance on a test.

   a. What is the examinee's true score on the five-item test with item parameters given in Table 3.1?

   b. An examinee must answer at least four items on this test correctly to be considered a master. Would this examinee be considered a master?

   c. What is the cut-off score in part b on the $\theta$ scale?

4. For a two-parameter model,

   a. show that the odds for success, $O$, is

$$O = e^{Da(\theta - b)}$$

   b. The odds for success on an item for two examinees with ability $\theta_1$ and $\theta_2$ are $O_1$ and $O_2$, respectively. Show that the odds ratio for the two examinees is

$$\frac{O_1}{O_2} = e^{Da(\theta_1 - \theta_2)}$$

   c. If the abilities of the examinees differ by one unit, what is the value of the odds ratio? What is the log of the odds ratio?

   d. What is the value of the odds ratio and the log of the odds ratio if the examinees differ by $k$ units?

## Answers to Exercises for Chapter 5

1. a. $y = 100(\theta + 4)$.

   b. $y = \dfrac{100}{n} \displaystyle\sum_{j=1}^{n} P_j(\theta)$

2. a. $\pi$ is a monotonically increasing function of $\theta$. It is bounded between 0.09 and 1. In fact, $\pi(\theta)$ looks like an item characteristic curve.

   b. The graph shows that the examinee with ability 1.2 has a domain score less than 0.8. Hence, the examinee may not be considered a master.

   c. From the graph, $\pi = 0.8$ corresponds to $\theta = 1.45$.

3.  a. $\tau = \Sigma P_i (\theta = 1.5) = 4.5$.

    b. Yes.

    c. $\theta = 1$.

4.  a. $Q(\theta) = 1 / [1 + e^{Da(\theta - b)}]$. Hence, $O = P / Q = e^{Da(\theta - b)}$

    b. $O_1 = e^{Da(\theta_1 - b)}$, $O_2 = e^{Da(\theta_2 - b)}$. Hence,

    $$O_1 / O_2 = e^{Da(\theta_1 - b)} / e^{Da(\theta_2 - b)} = e^{Da(\theta_1 - b) - Da(\theta_2 - b)} = e^{Da(\theta_1 - \theta_2)}$$

    c. If $\theta_2 - \theta_1 = 1$, then $O_1 / O_2 = e^{Da}$; $\ln(O_1 / O_2) = Da$.

    d. If $\theta_1 - \theta_2 = k$, then $O_1 / O_2 = e^{Dak}$; $\ln(O_1 / O_2) = Dak$.

# 6

# Item and Test Information and Efficiency Functions

## Basic Concepts

A powerful method of describing items and tests, selecting test items, and comparing tests is provided by item response theory. The method involves the use of *item information functions,* denoted $I_i(\theta)$, where

$$I_i(\theta) = \frac{[P_i^{'}(\theta)]^2}{P_i(\theta) Q_i(\theta)} \qquad i = 1, 2, \ldots, n \qquad [6.1]$$

$I_i(\theta)$ is the "information" provided by item $i$ at $\theta$, $P_i^{'}(\theta)$ is the derivative of $P_i(\theta)$ with respect to $\theta$, $P_i(\theta)$ is the item response function, and $Q_i(\theta) = 1 - P_i(\theta)$. Equation 6.1 applies to dichotomously scored logistic item response models like those given in Equations 2.1 to 2.3. In the case of the three-parameter logistic model, Equation 6.1 simplifies to (Birnbaum, 1968, chapter 17)

$$I_i(\theta) = \frac{2.89\, a_i^2 (1 - c_i)}{[c_i + e^{1.7 a_i (\theta - b_i)}]\, [1 + e^{-1.7 a_i (\theta - b_i)}]^2} \qquad [6.2]$$

From Equation 6.2 it is relatively easy to infer the role of the $b$, $a$, and $c$ parameters in the item information function: (a) information is higher when the $b$ value is close to $\theta$ than when the $b$ value is far from $\theta$, (b) information is generally higher when the $a$ parameter is high, and (c) information increases as the $c$ parameter goes to zero.

Item information functions can play an important role in test development and item evaluation in that they display the contribution items make to ability estimation at points along the ability continuum. This contribution depends to a great extent on an item's discriminating power (the higher it is, the steeper the slope of $P_i$), and the location at which this contribution will be realized is dependent on the item's difficulty. Birnbaum (1968) showed that an item provides its maximum information at $\theta_{max}$ where

$$\theta_{max} = b_i + \frac{1}{Da_i} \ln [0.5 (1 + \sqrt{1 + 8c_i}\,)]. \qquad [6.3]$$

If guessing is minimal, that is, $c_i = 0$, then $\theta_{max} = b_i$. In general, when $c_i > 0$, an item provides its maximum information at an ability level slightly higher than its difficulty.

The utility of item information functions in test development and evaluation depends on the fit of the item characteristic curves (ICCs) to the test data. If the fit of the ICCs to the data is poor, then the corresponding item statistics and item information functions will be misleading. Even when the fit is good, an item may have limited value in *all* tests if the *a* parameter is low and the *c* parameter is high. Moreover, the usefulness of test items (or tasks) will depend on the specific needs of the test developer within a given test. An item may provide considerable information at one end of the ability continuum but be of no value if information is needed elsewhere on the ability scale.

## Examples

Figure 6.1 shows the item information functions for the six test items presented in Figure 2.4 and Table 2.1. Figure 6.1 highlights several important points:

1. Maximum information provided by an item is at its difficulty level or slightly higher when $c > 0$. (This is seen by comparing the point on the ability scale where information is greatest to the *b* values of the corresponding items.)
2. The item discrimination parameter substantially influences the amount of information for assessing ability that is provided by an item. (This can be seen by comparing the item information functions for Items 1 and 2.)

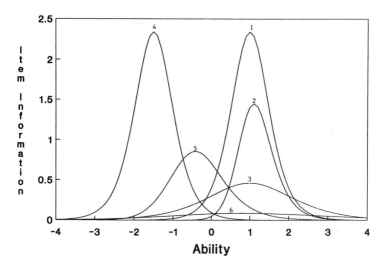

**Figure 6.1.** Item Information Functions for Six Typical Test Items

3. When $c > 0$, other things being equal, an item is less useful for assessing ability. (This can be seen by comparing the item information functions for Items 1 and 3.)
4. An item with low discriminating power is nearly useless statistically in a test (see Item 6).
5. Even the most discriminating items (Items 1 and 4) provide less information for assessing ability in some regions of the ability continuum than do less discriminating items (Item 5). Item 5 would be more useful for assessing abilities of middle-ability examinees than (say) either Item 1 or Item 4.

Clearly, item information functions provide new directions for judging the utility of test items and constructing tests.

Because item information functions are lower, generally, when $c > 0$ than when $c = 0$, researchers might be tempted to consider fitting one- or two-parameter models to their test data. Resulting item information functions will be higher; however, the one- and two-parameter item information curves will only be useful when the ICCs from which they are derived fit the test data. The use of ICCs that do not adequately fit the test data and their corresponding item information curves is far from optimal and will give misleading results (see, for example, de Gruijter, 1986).

## Test Information Functions

The information function for a test, denoted $I\theta$ and derived by Birnbaum (1968, chapter 17), is given by

$$I(\theta) = \sum_{i=1}^{n} I_i(\theta) \qquad [6.4]$$

The information provided by a test at $\theta$ is simply the sum of the item information functions at $\theta$. From Equation 6.4 it is clear that items contribute independently to the test information function. Thus, the contribution of individual test items can be determined without knowledge of the other items in the test. This feature is not available in classical test theory procedures. The contribution of test items to test reliability and item discrimination indices (e.g., point-biserial correlations) cannot be determined independently of the characteristics of the remaining items in the test. This is true because the test score, which is used in these calculations, is dependent on the particular selection of test items. Changing even one item will have an effect on test scores and, hence, all of the classical item and test indices will change.

The amount of information provided by a test at $\theta$ is inversely related to the precision with which ability is estimated at that point:

$$SE(\hat{\theta}) = \frac{1}{\sqrt{I(\theta)}} \qquad [6.5]$$

where $SE(\hat{\theta})$ is called the *standard error of estimation*. This result holds whenever maximum likelihood estimates of $\theta$ are obtained. With knowledge of the test information at $\theta$, a confidence band can be found for use in interpreting the ability estimate (see chapter 3). In the framework of IRT, $SE(\hat{\theta})$ serves the same role as the standard error of measurement in classical measurement theory. It is important to note, however, that the value of $SE(\hat{\theta})$ varies with ability level, whereas the classical standard error of measurement does not.

The standard error of $\hat{\theta}$, $SE(\hat{\theta})$, is the standard deviation of the asymptotically normal distribution of the maximum likelihood estimate of ability for a given true value of ability $\theta$. The distribution is normal when the test is long. Even with tests as short as 10 to 20 items, however, the normal approximation is satisfactory for most purposes (Samejima, 1977).

The magnitude of the standard error depends, in general, on (a) the number of test items (smaller standard errors are associated with longer tests); (b) the quality of test items (in general, smaller standard errors are associated with highly discriminating items for which the correct answers cannot be obtained by guessing); and (c) the match between item difficulty and examinee ability (smaller standard errors are associated with tests composed of items with difficulty parameters approximately equal to the ability parameter of the examinee, as opposed to tests that are relatively easy or relatively difficult). The size of the standard error quickly stabilizes, so that increasing information beyond a value of (say) 25, has only a small effect on the size of errors in ability estimation (see, for example, Green, Yen, & Burket, 1989).

## Relative Efficiency

Test developers are interested sometimes in comparing the information functions for two or more tests that measure the same ability. For example, a committee assigned the task of developing a national achievement test may want to compare the test information functions provided by tests composed of different items or exercises. Comparing information functions for two or more tests can serve as an aid in test evaluation and selection (see, for example, Lord, 1977). Another example would be a school district or state department of education interested in choosing a standardized achievement test. Based on prior information about student performance, the test that provides the most information in the region of the ability scale of interest would be preferred. (Other factors, however, should be taken into account in the selection of tests, such as validity, cost, content, and test length.)

The comparison of information functions is done by computing the relative efficiency of one test, compared with the other, as an estimator of ability at $\theta$:

$$RE(\theta) = \frac{I_A(\theta)}{I_B(\theta)} \qquad [6.6]$$

where $RE(\theta)$ denotes relative efficiency and $I_A(\theta)$ and $I_B(\theta)$ are the information functions for Tests A and B, respectively, defined over a common ability scale, $\theta$. If, for example, $I_A(\theta) = 25.0$ and $I_B(\theta) = 20.0$, then $RE(\theta) = 1.25$, and it is said that at $\theta$, Test A is functioning as if it were 25% longer than Test B. Then, Test B would need to be lengthened by 25% (by adding comparable items to those items already in the test) to yield the same precision of measurement as Test A at $\theta$. Alternatively, Test A could be shortened by 20% and still produce estimates of ability at $\theta$ possessing the same precision as estimates produced by Test B. These conclusions concerning the lengthening and shortening of tests are based on the assumption that items (or tasks) added or deleted are comparable in statistical quality to other items (or tasks) in the test. In the next chapter, two examples involving item and test information functions and relative efficiency are presented.

### Exercises for Chapter 6

1. a. For each of the six items given in Table 2.1, determine the value of $\theta$ for which the information function is a maximum, and determine the maximum value of the information.

   b. Which items would you choose to make up a two-item test that will be most useful for making decisions about examinees at $\theta = 1.0$? What is the value of the test information function for the two-item test at this value of $\theta$?

2. a. Show that if

$$P = \frac{1}{1 + e^{-1.7a(\theta - b)}}$$

   then

$$e^{1.7a(\theta - b)} = \frac{P}{Q}$$

   where $Q = 1 - P$.

b. Show that the expression given by Equation 6.2 may be written as

$$I(\theta) = \frac{2.89a^2(1 - c)P^2}{\left( c + \dfrac{P}{Q} \right)}$$

c. Deduce that for the two-parameter model,

$$I(\theta) = 2.89a^2PQ$$

3. Item parameters for an "item bank" made up of four items are given in Table 6.1.

**TABLE 6.1**

| Item | a | b | c |
|------|------|------|------|
| 1 | 1.25 | −0.5 | 0.00 |
| 2 | 1.50 | 0.0 | 0.00 |
| 3 | 1.25 | 1.0 | 0.00 |
| 4 | 1.00 | 1.5 | 0.00 |

Suppose it is necessary to construct a test made up of three items from this bank. Compute the test information function at $\theta$ values of −2, −1, 0, 1, 2 for the four three-item tests that can be constructed from the bank. Plot the four test information functions. Which set of items would you use if the test is designed as a mastery test with a cut-score set at $\theta = 1.0$?

## Answers to Exercises for Chapter 6

1. a. See Table 6.2.

**TABLE 6.2**

| Item | b | a | c | $\theta_{max} = b + \dfrac{1}{Da}\ln[0.5(1 + \sqrt{1 + 8c})]$ | $I(\theta_{max})$ |
|------|------|------|------|------|------|
| 1 | 1.0 | 1.8 | 0.00 | 1.00 | 2.34 |
| 2 | 1.0 | 0.8 | 0.00 | 1.00 | 0.46 |
| 3 | 1.0 | 1.8 | 0.25 | 1.10 | 1.29 |
| 4 | −1.5 | 1.8 | 0.00 | −1.50 | 2.34 |
| 5 | −0.5 | 1.2 | 0.10 | −0.42 | 0.85 |
| 6 | 0.5 | 0.4 | 0.15 | 0.82 | 1.03 |

b. Since Items 1 and 2 have their maximum information at $\theta = 1$, these would be the items of choice. Item 2 contributes much less than Item 1, and, hence, Item 1 may be sufficient.

2.  a. If $P = \dfrac{1}{1 + e^{-1.7a(\theta - b)}} = \dfrac{e^{1.7a(\theta - b)}}{1 + e^{1.7a(\theta - b)}}$

then $Q = 1 - P = \dfrac{1}{1 + e^{1.7a(\theta - b)}}$.

Hence, $1 + e^{1.7a(\theta - b)} = 1 / Q$, from which it follows that

$$e^{1.7a(\theta - b)} = \frac{1}{Q} - 1 = \frac{1 - Q}{Q} = \frac{P}{Q}$$

b. This follows directly from Expression 6.2 and part a.

c. For the two-parameter model, $c = 0$. Hence, from part b

$$I(\theta) = \frac{2.89a^2 P^2}{P / Q} = 2.89a^2 PQ$$

3.  See Table 6.3.

**TABLE 6.3**

| $\theta$ | Test (1, 2, 3) | Test (1, 2, 4) | Test (1, 3, 4) | Test (2, 3, 4) |
|---|---|---|---|---|
| -2 | 0.219 | 0.219 | 0.187 | 0.054 |
| -1 | 1.361 | 1.339 | 0.965 | 0.540 |
| 0 | 2.918 | 2.681 | 1.486 | 2.250 |
| 1 | 1.738 | 1.215 | 1.907 | 2.172 |
| 2 | 0.492 | 0.667 | 1.059 | 1.076 |

The test consisting of Items 2, 3, and 4 would be the most useful since it gives the most information at $\theta = 1.0$.

# 7

---

# Test Construction

## Background

The construction of achievement and aptitude tests using classical test theory techniques involves the selection of items according to their content and characteristics—item difficulty and discrimination. Items with high discriminating power are generally the most desirable, and the appropriate level of item difficulty is determined by the purpose of the test and the anticipated ability distribution of the group for whom the test is intended.

As noted in earlier chapters, classical indices are not invariant over populations that differ in ability. Hence, the success of classical item selection techniques depends on how closely the group used to determine the item indices matches the population for whom the test is intended. When the match is poor, the item indices obtained will not be appropriate for the intended population.

In many practical situations, the group for which item indices are obtained and the group for whom the test is intended are quite different. Consider, for example, the common practice in school districts of field-testing items in the fall for use in year-end tests in May or June. While such a field test is useful for detecting gross flaws in the items, the item indices themselves are not likely to be very useful in test development because the ability distribution of the students tested in the fall will differ substantially from the ability distribution of the students tested at the end of the school year.

Another situation in which classical item indices are obtained for groups that may differ from the intended population is in item banking. In developing an item bank, the characteristics of the items to be stored in the bank must be determined. In practice, these items, often called "experimental" items, are embedded in a test and administered to a group of examinees so that their item indices can be obtained. If the experimental items are numerous, obviously not all can be embedded in one test. Multiple forms of the test are created, each containing different experimental items and different forms are administered to different groups of examinees. It is usually not possible to ensure that the different forms are administered to equivalent groups; hence, the item indices for experimental items that were given to different groups of examinees may not be comparable. If the items are banked with the assumption that the item indices are comparable, any test constructed from the bank will not be appropriate for a given population.

Apart from the problem of noninvariant item indices, the major drawback of classical procedures for test construction is that even when a well-constructed item bank is available, items cannot be selected to yield a test that meets a fixed specification in terms of precision of measurement. The contribution of an item to the reliability of the test does not depend on the characteristics of the item alone, but also on the relationship between the item and the other items in the test. Thus, it is not possible to isolate the contribution of an item to the reliability and, hence, to the standard error of measurement of a test.

Item response theory offers a more powerful method of item selection than does classical test theory. Item parameters are invariant, overcoming the problems of classical item indices described above. In addition, item difficulty and examinee ability are measured on the same scale, making it possible to select items that are most useful in certain regions of the ability scale; for example, at a cut-off score for separating masters and nonmasters. Perhaps the most important advantage of IRT is that it permits the selection of items based on the amount of information the items contribute to the total amount of information needed in the test to meet the test specifications. Since information is related to precision of measurement, it is possible to choose items to produce a test that has the desired precision of measurement at any ability level, for example, at a cut-off score.


## Basic Approach

A procedure for using item information functions to build tests to meet any desired set of test specifications was outlined by Lord (1977). The procedure employs an item bank with item parameter estimates available for the IRT model of choice, with accompanying information functions.

The steps in the procedure suggested by Lord (1977) are as follows:

1. Decide on the shape of the desired test information function. This was termed the *target information function* by Lord (1977).
2. Select items from the item bank with item information functions that will fill up hard-to-fill areas under the target information function.
3. After each item is added to the test, calculate the test information function for the selected test items.
4. Continue selecting test items until the test information function approximates the target information function to a satisfactory degree.

These steps are implemented usually within a framework defined by the content specifications of the test.

For a broad-range ability test, the target information function should be fairly flat, reflecting the desire to produce a test that would provide (approximately) equally precise ability estimates over the ability scale. For a criterion-referenced test with a cut-off score to separate masters and nonmasters, the desired target information function should be highly peaked near the cut-off score on the ability scale.

The use of item information functions allows the test developer to produce a test that precisely fulfills any set of test specifications (assuming that the item bank is sufficiently large and contains items of high quality). An example of how item information functions can be applied in a large test-development project was given by Yen (1983). A procedure for automating item selection to match a test information function, where constraints can be placed on the resulting test to ensure content validity, desired length, and other characteristics, has been developed recently by van der Linden and Boekkooi-Timminga (1989).

Using the procedure suggested by Lord (1977) with a pool of items known to fit a particular item response model, it is possible to construct a test that "discriminates" well at a particular region of the ability continuum; that is, if we have a good idea of the ability level of a group of examinees, test items can be selected to maximize test information in the region of ability spanned by the examinees being measured. This selection of test items will contribute optimally to the precision with which ability parameters are estimated.

As an illustration of the above procedure, consider an achievement test. On achievement tests, it is common to observe lower performance on a pretest than on a posttest. Knowing this, the test constructor might select easier items for the pretest and more difficult items for the posttest. On each testing occasion, precision of measurement will be maximized in the region of ability where the examinees would most likely be located. Moreover, because the items on both tests measure the same ability and ability estimates do *not* depend on the particular choice of items, growth can be measured by subtracting the pretest ability estimate from the posttest ability estimate.

Investigations of the effects of optimal item selection on the decision-making accuracy of a test when the intended cut-off scores or standards for the test are known in advance of test development were conducted by de Gruijter and Hambleton (1983) and Hambleton and de Gruijter (1983). To provide a baseline for interpreting the results, tests were constructed also by selecting test items on a random basis. Random item selection from pools of acceptable test items is a common practice in criterion-referenced testing. Error rates (probabilities of misclassification) for the test constructed by random item selection procedures were nearly double the error rates obtained with the optimally selected test items. Optimal item selection is made possible within an IRT framework because items, persons, and cut-off scores are reported on the same scale.

The scenario simulated in the Hambleton and de Gruijter studies is not uncommon in testing practice. For example, in the summer of 1990, a group of educators and noneducators from the United States set standards for marginally basic, proficient, and advanced Grade 4 students on the 1990 NAEP Mathematics Assessment. These three standards were mapped onto the NAEP Reporting (Ability) Scale using the test characteristic function defined for the total pool of Grade 4 mathematics items. In 1991, when test items are selected for the 1992 Mathematics Assessment, test items could be chosen to maximize the test information at each of the standards. In this way, more accurate information about the percentage of students in each of the four ability intervals defined by the three standards could be obtained. Similar procedures could be used for the Grades 8 and 12 NAEP Mathematics Assessments.

A discussion of the process of setting target information functions and selecting items was provided by Kingston and Stocking (1986).

Several problems, however, remain to be addressed. One problem is that use of statistical criteria for item selection alone will not ensure a content-valid test. Unfortunately, it is easy to overemphasize statistical criteria and not take into account the important role that item content plays in test development. Failure to attend to content considerations might result in a charge that the test lacks content validity. Ways must be found to combine information about item content and statistical criteria in the item selection process. A solution to this problem has been provided by van der Linden and Boekkooi-Timminga (1989), using linear programming techniques.

Another problem in using item information functions in test development is that high $a$ values are likely to be overestimated and, hence, the information function may be biased. A test constructed using items with high $a$ values is likely to be different from the expected test (see, for example, Hambleton, Jones, & Rogers, 1990). Since the test information function will be overestimated, adding several extra items to the test will compensate for the overestimation. A better solution is to strive for large examinee samples so that accurate item parameter estimates can be obtained.

Two examples of the use of information functions in the construction of tests for specific purposes are given below.

### Example 1: Broad Abilities Test

Suppose the test developer's intent is to produce a wide-range ability test using the item bank in the Appendix. Suppose also that standard errors of (approximately) 0.50 would be acceptable in the ability range (–2.00, 2.00), with somewhat larger errors outside that interval. A possible target information function is shown in Figure 7.1. If $SE(\hat{\theta}) = 0.50$, then $I(\theta) = 4.00$. To construct the shortest possible test that meets the target, items with high discriminations, difficulties between –2.00 and +2.00, and low $c$ values must be chosen. Figure 7.1 shows the target information function (which is flat, with $I(\theta) = 4.00$ between $\theta = -2$ and $\theta = 2$) and the test information functions after selecting the best 10, 15, and 20 test items from the item bank for the desired test. Clearly, the resulting 20-item test fairly closely approximates the desired test. The addition of items with difficulties near –2 and 2 would produce an even better match to the target information function.

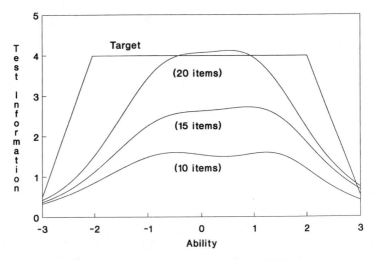

**Figure 7.1.** Test Information Functions for 10, 15, and 20 Test Items

## Example 2: Criterion-Referenced Test Construction

Suppose the test developer wishes to construct a 15-item criterion-referenced test (drawn from the item pool shown in the Appendix) to provide maximum information at the cut-off score $\theta = -0.50$. The resulting test information function is shown in Figure 7.2. The items selected were 2, 3, 5, 7, 14, 24, 27, 30, 32, 36, 47, 48, 71, 72, and 73. (Others were possible, but these 15 ultimately were chosen.) For the purposes of comparison, a 15-item test (called the *standard test*) was constructed by drawing items at random (a common practice in criterion-referenced test development) and the test information function for this test also is shown in Figure 7.2. Figure 7.3 shows the relative efficiency of the optimal test compared with the standard test. Clearly, the optimal test provides greater measurement precision in the region of the cut-off score ($\theta = -0.50$). The optimal test performs about 60% better than the standard test in this region. The standard test would need to be lengthened from 15 to 24 test items to perform approximately as well as the optimal test.

As can be seen in Figures 7.2 and 7.3, the optimal test does not perform as well as the standard test for high-ability examinees. This is

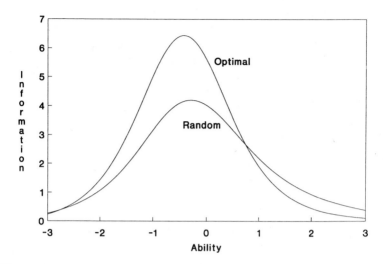

**Figure 7.2.** Test Information Functions for 15-Item Optimal and Randomly Constructed Tests

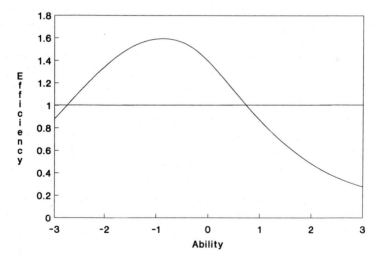

**Figure 7.3.** Efficiency Function for 15-Item Optimal Versus Randomly Constructed Tests

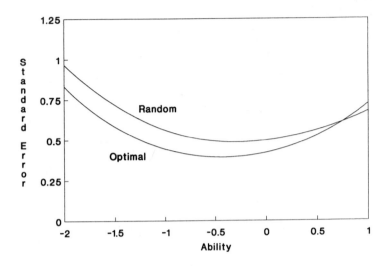

**Figure 7.4.** Standard Error Functions for 15-Item Optimal and Randomly Constructed Tests

due to the fact that the optimal test is composed largely of items that discriminate near the cut-off score and does not contain many items that are suitable for high-ability examinees. The standard test includes a more heterogeneous selection of test items.

In practice, the more heterogeneous the item pool and the shorter the test of interest in relation to the size of the item pool, the greater the advantages of optimal item selection over random item selection. The standard errors corresponding to the information functions for the two tests are shown in Figure 7.4.

### Exercises for Chapter 7

1. Suppose you have an item bank containing six test items that provide information at various $\theta$ values as shown in Table 7.1.
   a. What is the test information and corresponding standard error at $\theta = 1.0$ for a test consisting of Items 2, 3, and 6?
   b. How many items like Item 5 are needed to obtain a standard error of 0.40 at $\theta = -1.0$?

**TABLE 7.1**

| Item | θ | | | | | | |
|------|-----|------|------|------|------|------|------|
| | −3 | −2 | −1 | 0 | 1 | 2 | 3 |
| 1 | .02 | 0.06 | 0.10 | 0.20 | 0.15 | 0.08 | 0.04 |
| 2 | .00 | 0.00 | 0.05 | 0.10 | 1.10 | 0.25 | 0.10 |
| 3 | .00 | 0.03 | 0.10 | 0.25 | 0.50 | 0.40 | 0.15 |
| 4 | .15 | 1.25 | 1.45 | 0.10 | 0.02 | 0.00 | 0.00 |
| 5 | .00 | 0.10 | 0.60 | 0.70 | 0.20 | 0.05 | 0.00 |
| 6 | .00 | 0.00 | 0.02 | 0.40 | 2.20 | 0.40 | 0.15 |

2. Two tests are constructed from the item bank given in Exercise 1. Test 1 consists of Items 2 and 3; Test 2 consists of Items 1 and 6.

   a. Compute the information provided by each test at $\theta = 0.0$, 1.0, and 2.0.

   b. Compute the efficiency of Test 1 relative to Test 2 at $\theta = 0.0$, 1.0, and 2.0.

   c. What does the relative efficiency analysis indicate about Test 1?

   d. How many items like Item 5 need to be added to Test 1 so that Tests 1 and 2 are (approximately) equally informative at $\theta = 1.0$?

3. Suppose that it is desired to construct a criterion-referenced test that is optimally discriminating at $\theta = -1.0$.

   a. If the test consists of Items 4 and 5, what is the standard error at $\theta = -1.0$?

   b. What is the probability that a candidate with $\theta = 0.0$ will fail the test when the cut-off score is set at $\theta = -1.0$?

## Answers to Exercises for Chapter 7

1. a. $I(\theta = 1.0) = 3.8$; $SE(\theta = 1.0) = 0.51$.

   b. $SE = 0.40$ requires $I(\theta) = 6.25$. Since the information at $\theta = -1.0$ is 0.60, 11 items like Item 5 are required to produce the desired test.

2. a. See Table 7.2.

   **TABLE 7.2**

| Test | θ | | |
|------|-----|-----|-----|
| | 0.0 | 1.0 | 2.0 |
| 1 (Items 2 and 3) | 0.35 | 1.60 | 0.65 |
| 2 (Items 1 and 6) | 0.60 | 2.35 | 0.48 |

b. See Table 7.3.

**TABLE 7.3**

| Test | θ 0.0 | 1.0 | 2.0 |
|------|-------|-----|-----|
| Efficiency (1 vs. 2) | 0.58 | 0.68 | 1.35 |

c. Test 1 is providing about 58% as much information as Test 2 at $\theta = 0.0$, and about 68% as much information as Test 2 at $\theta = 1.0$. At $\theta = 2.0$, Test 1 is providing more information than Test 2.

d. 4

3. a. $SE(\theta = -1.0) = 0.70$

b. The standard error of ability estimation at $\theta = 0.0$ is 1.12. Therefore, the probability of this candidate failing the test (i.e., the probability of making a false-negative error) is 0.197.

# 8

---

## Identification of Potentially Biased
## Test Items

### Background

Perhaps the most highly charged issue surrounding testing, and certainly the one of greatest importance to the public, is that of test fairness. Claims that tests are biased against racial or ethnic minorities have led to numerous lawsuits and calls by such organizations as the NAACP for moratoria or bans on certain types of tests (Rudner, Getson, & Knight, 1980). Tests and testing practices have come under close public scrutiny, and test publishers and users must demonstrate now that their tests are free of bias against minorities. One of the desirable features of item response theory is that it provides a unified framework for conceptualizing and investigating bias at the item level.

Before IRT procedures for investigating bias can be discussed, some clarification of terminology is necessary. Investigations of bias involve gathering *empirical* evidence concerning the relative performances on the test item of members of the minority group of interest and members of the group that represents the majority. Empirical evidence of differential performance is necessary, but not sufficient, to draw the conclusion that bias is present; this conclusion involves an inference that goes beyond the data. To distinguish the empirical evidence from the conclusion, the term *differential item functioning* (DIF) rather than *bias* is used commonly to described the empirical evidence obtained in investigations of bias.

Some argument exists as to the appropriate definition of DIF. A definition that has been used in recent legal settlements and legislation concerning fair testing is that "an item shows DIF if the majority and minority groups differ in their mean performances on the item." The problem with this definition is that it does not take into account the possibility that other variables, such as a real between-group difference in ability, may be responsible for the difference in $p$-values (see Lord, 1980).

The definition of DIF accepted by psychometricians is that "an item shows DIF if individuals having the same ability, but from different groups, do not have the same probability of getting the item right."

## IRT Methods for Detecting DIF

Given the accepted definition of DIF, item response theory provides a natural framework for studying DIF. Since the item characteristic function relates the probability of a correct response to the underlying ability and to the characteristics of the item, the definition of DIF may be restated operationally as follows: "An item shows DIF if the item response functions across different subgroups are not identical. Conversely, an item does not show DIF if the item characteristic functions across different subgroups are identical."

Based on the definition given above, DIF may be investigated by comparing the item characteristic functions of two or more groups. Item characteristic functions may be compared in several ways. The first and, intuitively, most direct approach is to compare the parameters that describe the item characteristic curves. Since the ICCs are completely determined by their corresponding item parameters, two ICCs can be different only if the item parameters that describe them are different (Lord, 1980). A second approach is to compare the ICCs by evaluating the area between them (Rudner et al., 1980). If the area between the ICCs is zero, then the ICCs coincide and, hence, no DIF is present. These two approaches for studying DIF are described in the following sections.

*Comparison of Item Parameters.* If the parameters of two item characteristic functions are identical, then the functions will be identical at all points and the probabilities of a correct response will be the same. The null hypothesis that the item response functions are the same may be stated as

$$H_0: \quad b_1 = b_2; \quad a_1 = a_2; \quad c_1 = c_2$$

where the subscript denotes the group in which the parameter estimates were obtained. If the hypothesis is rejected for a given item, we can conclude that DIF is present for that item.

To test the null hypothesis, estimates of the item parameters and the variance–covariance matrices of the estimates are needed. Recall that when estimating item and ability parameters in each group, a scale for the parameters must be specified (chapter 3); this is done typically by standardizing either the ability estimates or the difficulty estimates in each group. As we shall see later (chapter 9), standardizing the ability estimates usually will result in different scales in each group, and the item parameter estimates will not be on a common scale. Standardizing the difficulty parameters will result in item parameter estimates that are on a common scale.

After the item parameter estimates are placed on a common scale, the variance–covariance matrix of the parameter estimates in each group is computed. First, the information matrix is computed (see chapter 3) for each group and is inverted. The variance–covariance matrices of the two groups are added then to yield the variance–covariance matrix of the differences between the estimates. The statistic for testing the null hypothesis is

$$\chi^2 = (a_{\text{diff}} \ b_{\text{diff}} \ c_{\text{diff}})' \ \Sigma^{-1} \ (a_{\text{diff}} \ b_{\text{diff}} \ c_{\text{diff}})$$

where

$$a_{\text{diff}} = a_2 - a_1 \qquad b_{\text{diff}} = b_2 - b_1 \qquad c_{\text{diff}} = c_2 - c_1$$

and $\Sigma$ is the variance–covariance matrix of the differences between the parameter estimates. The test statistic is asymptotically (that is, in large samples) distributed as a chi-square with $p$ degrees of freedom, where $p$ is the number of parameters compared. For the three-parameter model, when $a$, $b$, and $c$ are compared for each item, $p = 3$; for the two-parameter model, $p = 2$; for the one-parameter model, $p = 1$. In the case of the one-parameter model, the expression for the chi-square statistic simplifies considerably; the test statistic in this case is

$$\chi^2 = \frac{b_{\text{diff}}^2}{v(b_1) + v(b_2)}$$

where $v(b_1)$ and $v(b_2)$ are the reciprocals of the information functions for the difficulty parameter estimates.

Since the $c$ parameter is often poorly estimated and, hence, has a large standard error, its inclusion in the test statistic may produce a very conservative test, that is, a test that is not powerful in detecting DIF. An alternative is to compare only the $a$ and $b$ parameters and to ignore the $c$ parameters. This approach is reasonable, since if differences exist in the $a$ and $b$ parameters across groups, then the item characteristic functions will be different, regardless of the $c$ parameter values; without differences in the $a$ and $b$ parameters, apparent differences between the $c$ parameters would be too unreliable to warrant the conclusion that the item characteristic functions are different (Lord, 1980).

The comparison of item parameters as a means of comparing item characteristic functions has been criticized on the grounds that significant differences between the parameters may be found when no practical differences exist between the ICCs in the ability range of interest. An example of item parameter values for two groups that produce almost identical ICCs in the ability range $(-3, 3)$ was given by Linn, Levine, Hastings, and Wardrop (1981). The item parameters for the two groups are given below:

$$\text{Group 1:} \quad a = 1.8; \quad b = 3.5; \quad c = 0.2$$
$$\text{Group 2:} \quad a = 0.5; \quad b = 5.0; \quad c = 0.2$$

Although significant differences exist between the parameters, the ICCs for the two groups differ by less than 0.05 in the specified ability range. It should be noted, however, that this item was extremely difficult for both groups and, hence, an inappropriate item for these groups. If the two ICCs were compared in the ability range for which this item is appropriate, a considerable difference between the ICCs would be observed. For items of appropriate difficulty for at least one of the two groups of examinees (items with difficulty parameters in the ability range of interest), it is *not* possible to obtain significant differences between the item parameters for the two groups without a corresponding difference in the ICCs.

A more valid criticism of the comparison of item parameters is that the distribution of the test statistic is known only asymptotically; furthermore, the asymptotic distribution is applicable only when item parameters are estimated in the presence of known ability parameters (Hambleton & Swaminathan, 1985). It is not known how large the sample size must be in order for the asymptotic distribution to apply, and it is not known whether the asymptotic distribution applies when item and ability parameters are estimated simultaneously. In addition to this problem, some evidence suggests that the chi-square statistic has a higher than expected false-positive rate (McLaughlin & Drasgow, 1987).

*Area Between Item Characteristic Curves.* An alternative approach to the comparison of item characteristic functions is to compare the ICCs themselves rather than their parameters. If, after placing the parameter estimates on a common scale, the ICCs are identical, then the area between them should be zero (Rudner et al., 1980); when the area between ICCs is not zero, we can conclude that DIF is present.

In computing the area, numerical procedures were used until recently. The numerical procedure involved (a) dividing the ability range into $k$ intervals, (b) constructing rectangles centered around the midpoint of each interval, (c) obtaining the values of the ICCs (the probabilities) at the midpoint of each interval, (d) taking the absolute value of the differences between the probabilities, and (e) multiplying the difference by the interval width and summing. Symbolically, this procedure may be expressed for item $i$ as

$$A_i = \sum_{\theta = r}^{s} |P_{i1}(\theta) - P_{i2}(\theta)| \Delta\theta$$

The quantity $\Delta\theta$ is the width of the interval and is chosen to be as small as possible (e.g., 0.01). The values $r$ and $s$ indicate the ability range over which the area is to be calculated; the range is arbitrary and is chosen by the user. A typical choice for the ability range would be the range from three standard deviations below the lower group mean ability to three standard deviations above the upper group mean ability. This choice ensures that the area is calculated over the ability range in which nearly all examinees fall.

Raju (1988) derived an exact expression for computing the area between the ICCs for the one-, two-, and three-parameter models. The expression for the three-parameter model is

$$\text{Area} = (1-c)\left| \frac{2(a_2 - a_1)}{D a_1 a_2} \ln[1 + e^{D a_1 a_2 (b_2 - b_1)/(a_2 - a_1)}] - (b_2 - b_1) \right|$$

For the two-parameter model, the term involving $c$ disappears; for the one-parameter model, the expression reduces to the absolute difference between the $b$-values for the two groups.

In the expression for the area given above, the value of the $c$ parameter is assumed to be the same for both groups. Raju (1988) has shown that when the $c$ parameters are not the same, the area between the two curves is infinite if calculated over the entire range of ability $(-\infty, \infty)$. For a finite range of ability, the area is finite; however, no expression has been derived for the area between ICCs in a finite ability range, and so numerical methods must be used.

Raju (1990) derived an expression for the standard error of the area statistic and suggested that the area statistic divided by its standard error can be taken as approximately normally distributed. This procedure is based on the assumption that the $c$ parameter values are the same for the two groups and are fixed (i.e., not estimated).

When the $c$ parameters for the two groups are not the same, the significance test for the area statistic cannot be carried out. The problem is to find a "cut-off" value for the area statistic that can be used to decide whether DIF is present. An empirical approach to determining a cut-off is to divide the group with the larger sample size into two randomly equivalent groups, to estimate the ICCs in each group separately, and to determine the area between the estimated ICCs (Hambleton & Rogers, 1989). Since the groups are randomly equivalent, the area should be zero. Nonzero values of the area statistic are regarded as resulting from sampling fluctuations, and the largest area value obtained may be regarded as the largest value that may be expected in terms of sampling fluctuation. Any area value greater than this is assumed to be "significant" and, consequently, indicative of DIF when the majority and minority groups are compared.

One disadvantage of the approach to establishing the cut-off value described above is that, as a result of halving the sample, the parameter estimates may be unstable; consequently, the area statistic may not be a reliable indicator of DIF. An alternative approach is to use simulated data to establish the cut-off value (Rogers & Hambleton, 1989). In this approach, the two groups of interest are combined and parameters are estimated for the total group. The item parameter estimates for the total group and the ability parameter estimates for the majority group are used to generate a set of data of the same size as the majority group. Similarly, the item parameter estimates for the total group and the ability parameter estimates for the minority group are used to generate a set of data of the same size as the minority group. The two sets of simulated data closely resemble the data for the majority and minority groups in terms of sample sizes, distributions of ability, and item characteristics. The one difference is that the two sets of simulated data are based on the same item parameters and, hence, no DIF is present. Item and ability parameters then are estimated separately for each set of simulated data, and area statistics are computed for each item. Since no DIF is present, nonzero area values are the result of sampling fluctuations; as described above, the largest area value obtained in this comparison may be regarded as a cut-off value for use in the comparison of ICCs for the real majority and minority groups.

The empirical procedure described above for establishing critical values may capitalize on chance because only one replication is performed. Multiple replications may be carried out and a cut-off value might be established for each item; however, such a procedure would be so computer-intensive as to be prohibitive.

A problem common to the IRT approaches described above is that item parameters must be estimated in both groups. For proper estimation, a large number of examinees with a large ability range is needed. In typical DIF studies, the number of examinees in the minority group is usually small (around 300); furthermore, the group may have a restricted ability range. Since item parameters will be estimated poorly in such situations, the DIF statistics may lead to erroneous decisions about the presence of DIF.

Because of the problems associated with IRT methods for detecting DIF, alternative methods have been sought. The most popular of the current non-IRT approaches for detecting DIF is the Mantel–Haenszel method (Holland & Thayer, 1988). Unfortunately, this method is not sensitive to nonuniform DIF. More recently, Swaminathan and Rogers (1990) have provided a logistic regression procedure capable of detecting nonuniform, as well as uniform, DIF.

## Example

The IRT approaches to the investigation of bias described in this chapter are illustrated using the New Mexico data set introduced in chapter 4. In this example the majority group is Anglo-American and the minority group is Native American. For the purposes of the example, a random sample of 1,000 Anglo-Americans and a random sample of 1,000 Native Americans were drawn from the total set of data.

Three-parameter item response models were fitted separately to the item responses of each of the two groups. In computing the parameter estimates, the metric was fixed by standardizing the $b$ values. Since the two sets of data consisted of responses to the same items, standardizing the $b$ values in each group automatically placed the item parameter estimates for the two groups on the same scale.

Area statistics were computed for each item. Because the $c$ values for the two groups were unequal for most items, the numerical method of calculating the area values was used. The $\theta$ increment used in the calculations was 0.01. The area was calculated over the ability range from three standard deviations below the lower group mean $\theta$ to three standard deviations above the upper group mean $\theta$; the resulting ability range was (−3.36, 3.55).

Simulated data were used to determine the cut-off value, as described earlier. Item responses were simulated for two groups for which no item had DIF. To obtain parameter values for generating the item responses, the two groups were combined first and parameter estimates were computed for the total group (these parameter estimates are reported in the Appendix). The ability estimates for the majority group and the item parameter estimates for the combined group were used then to simulate a set of data resembling the majority group; similarly, the ability estimates for the minority group and the item parameter estimates for the combined group were used to simulate a set of data resembling the minority group. Since the same item parameters were used to generate the data for the two groups, the simulated data represent the situation that has no DIF.

Three-parameter models were fitted separately to each set of simulated data, with the metric fixed by standardizing the $b$ values in each group. Area statistics were computed for each item, and the largest area value obtained was used as the cut-off value in the Anglo-Native American comparison. The largest area value obtained in the simulated data comparison was 0.498.

In comparing the item parameters for the two groups, two chi-square statistics were calculated. The first chi-square statistic, denoted as $\chi^2_{ab}$, was based on only the $a$ and $b$ parameters for the two groups, while the second chi-square statistic, denoted as $\chi^2_{abc}$, was based on the $a$, $b$, and $c$ parameters. The second chi-square test was carried out primarily for

**TABLE 8.1** Item Parameter Estimates, Area Statistics, and $\chi^2$ Values for Twenty-Five Randomly Chosen Test Items

| | *Majority Group* | | | *Minority Group* | | | | *DIF Statistics* | |
| --- | --- | --- | --- | --- | --- | --- | --- | --- | --- |
| *Item* | $b_1$ | $a_1$ | $c_1$ | $b_2$ | $a_2$ | $c_2$ | *Area* | $\chi^2_{ab}$ [a] | $\chi^2_{abc}$ [b] |
| 1 | 0.840 | 0.575 | 0.190 | 0.823 | 0.896 | 0.170 | 0.417 | 5.84 | 6.01 |
| 3 | −0.412 | 0.773 | 0.190 | −0.008 | 0.906 | 0.170 | 0.388 | 7.90 | 9.52 |
| 5 | −1.347 | 0.413 | 0.190 | −0.953 | 0.821 | 0.170 | 0.609* | 21.13* | 12.99 |
| 8 | 0.125 | 0.608 | 0.190 | 0.286 | 0.414 | 0.170 | 0.344 | 5.31 | 5.21 |
| 11 | 0.319 | 0.639 | 0.190 | −0.197 | 0.645 | 0.170 | 0.342 | 17.80* | 14.74 |
| 13 | 0.693 | 0.714 | 0.190 | 0.728 | 0.303 | 0.170 | 0.732* | 21.86* | 19.38* |
| 14 | −0.308 | 1.044 | 0.190 | −0.650 | 0.551 | 0.170 | 0.494 | 17.12* | 15.83 |
| 16 | −0.193 | 0.977 | 0.190 | 0.286 | 1.999 | 0.231 | 0.405 | 29.13* | 23.07* |
| 20 | −0.337 | 0.536 | 0.190 | −0.106 | 0.595 | 0.170 | 0.238 | 1.57 | 2.42 |
| 21 | −0.514 | 0.529 | 0.190 | −0.628 | 0.407 | 0.170 | 0.217 | 2.20 | 2.22 |
| 30 | −1.463 | 0.488 | 0.190 | −0.716 | 0.839 | 0.170 | 0.637* | 11.14 | 9.78 |
| 38 | −1.168 | 0.549 | 0.190 | −1.175 | 0.433 | 0.170 | 0.195 | 4.15 | 4.64 |
| 41 | 1.011 | 0.849 | 0.190 | 0.943 | 1.054 | 0.170 | 0.214 | 1.33 | 1.76 |
| 45 | 1.808 | 1.166 | 0.137 | 2.778 | 0.509 | 0.125 | 0.641* | 14.74* | 12.08 |
| 46 | −0.481 | 0.583 | 0.190 | 0.140 | 0.586 | 0.170 | 0.540* | 11.62 | 13.09 |
| 49 | −0.663 | 0.661 | 0.190 | −1.128 | 0.528 | 0.170 | 0.290 | 5.73 | 3.64 |
| 50 | 0.409 | 0.431 | 0.190 | 0.265 | 0.430 | 0.170 | 0.057 | 0.56 | 0.15 |
| 52 | 1.444 | 1.050 | 0.190 | 1.246 | 1.201 | 0.137 | 0.315 | 1.94 | 3.19 |
| 56 | 0.338 | 0.404 | 0.190 | 1.545 | 0.405 | 0.170 | 0.880* | 14.11* | 16.42* |
| 57 | 0.281 | 0.685 | 0.190 | −0.497 | 0.489 | 0.170 | 0.536* | 32.43* | 21.54* |
| 60 | 0.904 | 0.569 | 0.190 | 1.154 | 0.531 | 0.170 | 0.257 | 1.19 | 2.10 |
| 64 | 0.245 | 0.442 | 0.190 | −0.387 | 0.280 | 0.170 | 0.467 | 10.52 | 5.56 |
| 68 | −1.398 | 0.340 | 0.190 | −0.122 | 0.683 | 0.170 | 0.942* | 15.41* | 15.07 |
| 73 | −0.567 | 0.640 | 0.190 | −0.007 | 1.223 | 0.170 | 0.648* | 20.29* | 20.04* |
| 75 | 1.646 | 0.317 | 0.190 | 0.534 | 0.562 | 0.170 | 0.722* | 23.53* | 15.24 |

a. $\chi^2_{2,.001} = 13.82$

b. $\chi^2_{3,.001} = 16.27$

*Significant at the 0.001 level

illustrative purposes. The significance level for each chi-square statistic was set at 0.001 to ensure that the overall Type I error rate was around 0.05. For the $\chi^2_{abc}$ statistic, the critical value was $\chi^2_{3,.001} = 16.27$; for the $\chi^2_{ab}$ statistic, the critical value was $\chi^2_{2,.001} = 13.82$.

The item parameters for the two groups, the area statistics, and the chi-square values for 25 randomly chosen items are reported in Table 8.1. Of the 75 items analyzed altogether, the area statistic flagged 20 items as showing DIF, while the $\chi^2_{ab}$ statistic flagged 25 items. The $\chi^2_{abc}$ statistic flagged only 9 items, which represented a subset of those

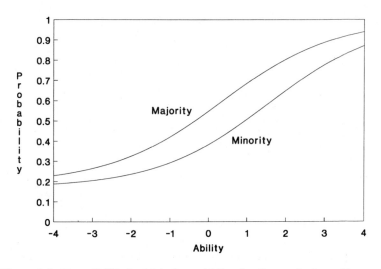

**Figure 8.1.** Plot of ICCs for Majority and Minority Groups for Item 56

flagged by the $\chi^2_{ab}$ statistic. As expected, the $\chi^2_{abc}$ statistic was more conservative than the $\chi^2_{ab}$ and area statistics.

The degree of agreement between the area and $\chi^2_{ab}$ chi-square statistics was moderate: 77% of the items were classified in the same way (either showing DIF or not) by the two methods. The rank order correlation between the two methods was 0.71. Two examples of items flagged by both procedures are given in Figures 8.1 and 8.2. These items differ in the type of DIF observed. In Figure 8.1, the ICCs for the two groups are more or less parallel, differing mainly in their *b* parameters. This type of DIF is referred to as *uniform DIF;* the difference in probabilities of success is uniform for the two groups over all ability levels. In Figure 8.2, the ICCs for the two groups cross; the probability of success is greater for the minority group than for the majority group at the low end of the ability scale, but is greater for the majority group at the high end of the ability scale. This type of DIF is referred to as *nonuniform DIF,* since the difference in probabilities is not uniform across ability levels. One of the advantages of IRT procedures for detecting DIF is their sensitivity to these different types of DIF; this feature is not shared by some of the popular non-IRT procedures

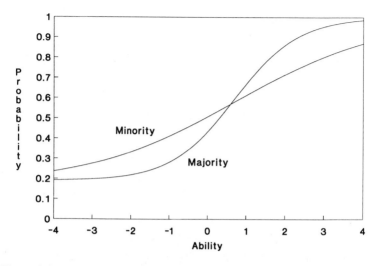

**Figure 8.2.** Plot of ICCs for Majority and Minority Groups for Item 13

for detecting DIF (Holland & Thayer, 1988; Swaminathan & Rogers, 1990).

Of the 20 items flagged by the $\chi^2_{ab}$ statistic, 6 were not flagged by the area statistic; 11 of the items flagged by the area statistic were not flagged by the $\chi^2_{ab}$ statistic. Examination of the ICCs for the items inconsistently flagged revealed no reason for the result. This finding demonstrates one of the problems of all methods for detecting DIF: while the agreement among methods is moderate, unexplainable differences occur often.

## Summary

Item response theory procedures for detecting DIF involve the comparison of item characteristic functions for two groups of interest. Two ways in which item characteristic functions may be compared are (a) by comparing their parameters or (b) by calculating the area between the curves. To compare item parameters for two groups, a chi-square statistic is computed. The statistic may or may not include the $c$ parameter;

the reason for not including $c$ is that it is often poorly estimated and, hence, is unreliable. An advantage of the chi-square statistic is that it has a known distribution; a possible disadvantage of the procedure is that it may have a high false-positive rate.

The area between ICCs can be computed using an exact expression when the $c$ parameters for the two groups are the same, and a significance test for the area is available in this case. When the $c$ parameters are not the same, numerical procedures must be used to calculate the area and no significance test is available. In this case an empirical "cut-off" value must be obtained. This is done using either randomly equivalent samples or simulated data in which there is no DIF. Area values are calculated for this comparison, and the largest value obtained is used as the cut-off for the real analysis.

Several other IRT approaches to the detection of DIF have not been described in this chapter. Linn and Harnisch (1981) suggested evaluating the fit in the minority group of the IRT model obtained in the total group. The procedure is carried out by estimating item and ability parameters for the combined majority–minority group; the item parameter estimates and the ability parameter estimates for the minority group obtained in the combined-group analysis are used to assess the fit of the model to the item response data for the minority group. If no DIF is found, the ICC obtained for the total group should fit the data for the minority group; if DIF is found, the parameters will not be invariant across the two groups and the model obtained for the total group will not fit the minority group. Goodness-of-fit statistics can be computed for each item to determine whether DIF is present. This procedure does not require the estimation of item parameters in the minority group (which is usually small) and, hence, overcomes some of the difficulties encountered in the two approaches described in this chapter.

Another procedure, suggested by Linn et al. (1981), is to calculate the sum of squared differences between the ICCs for every observed value of $\theta$. This procedure may be modified to take into account the error in the estimated probabilities (Shepard, Camilli, & Williams, 1985).

Several comparisons of the effectiveness of IRT and non-IRT methods for detecting DIF have been completed. The reader is referred to Mellenbergh (1989); Rudner et al. (1980); Shepard, Camilli, and Averill (1981); Shepard et al. (1985); and Subkoviak, Mack, Ironson, and Craig (1984).

## Exercises for Chapter 8

1. In an investigation of DIF, a one-parameter model was fitted to the data separately for the minority and majority groups. For a particular item, the difficulty parameter estimates and the standard errors for the two groups were computed and are given in Table 8.2.

**TABLE 8.2**

|  | Majority Group | Minority Group |
|---|---|---|
| Difficulty Estimate: | 0.34 | 0.89 |
| Standard Error: | 0.15 | 0.16 |

a. Compute the variance of each difficulty estimate.

b. Calculate the chi-square statistic for the difference between the difficulty estimates for the two groups.

c. Does it appear that this item functions differentially in the two groups?

2. In carrying out the DIF analysis on the New Mexico data set, the item parameter estimates for Item 43 contained in Table 8.3 were obtained in the Anglo-American and Native American groups.

**TABLE 8.3**

| Group | $a$ | $b$ | $c$ |
|---|---|---|---|
| Anglo-American | 0.93 | 0.90 | 0.2 |
| Native American | 0.42 | 1.82 | 0.2 |

a. Using the formula given by Raju (1988), calculate the area between the ICCs for the two groups. Explain why this formula can be used in this situation.

$$\text{Area} = (1-c) \left| \frac{2(a_2 - a_1)}{D a_1 a_2} \ln \left[ 1 + e^{D a_1 a_2 (b_2 - b_1)/(a_2 - a_1)} \right] - (b_2 - b_1) \right|$$

b. Using the cut-off value used in the example for the Anglo-American versus comparison (cut-off value = 0.468), determine if the item shows DIF.

## Answers to Exercises for Chapter 8

1. a. For majority group: variance = $SE^2 = 0.15^2 = 0.0225$
      For minority group: variance = $SE^2 = 0.16^2 = 0.0256$

   b. For the one-parameter model, the $\chi^2$ statistic simplifies:

   $$\chi^2 = \frac{(b_2 - b_1)^2}{var(b_1) + var(b_2)} = \frac{(0.89 - 0.34)^2}{0.0225 + 0.0256} = 6.29$$

   c. $\chi^2_{1, 0.05} = 3.84$. Since the calculated value exceeds the critical value, we can conclude that this item functions differentially in the two groups.

2. a. Area $= (1 - 0.2) \left| \dfrac{2(0.42 - 0.93)}{1.7 \times 0.42 \times 0.93} \times \right.$

   $$\left. \ln \left[ 1 + \exp \ \frac{1.7 \times 0.42 \times 0.93 \times (1.82 - 0.90)}{0.42 - 0.93} \right] - (1.82 - 0.90) \right|$$

   $$= 0.8 \times \left| -1.536 \ \ln [1 + \exp \ (-1.20)] - 0.92 \right| = 1.06$$

   The formula can be used because the $c$ values for the two groups are the same.

   b. The area value exceeds the cut-off value. We can conclude that the item shows DIF.

# 9

## Test Score Equating

### Background

The comparability of test scores across different tests measuring the same ability is an issue of considerable importance to test developers, measurement specialists, and test takers alike. If two examinees take different tests, how can their scores be compared? This question is particularly important when certification, selection, or pass-fail decisions must be made, since it should be a matter of indifference which test is used to make the decision.

To compare the scores obtained on tests X and Y, a process of *equating* scores on the two tests must be carried out. Through this process a correspondence between the scores on X and Y is established, and the score on test X is converted to the metric of test Y. Thus, an examinee who obtains a score $x$ on test X has a converted score $y^*$ on test Y; this score is comparable to the score $y$ of an examinee taking test Y. In making pass-fail, selection, or certification decisions, the cut-off score, $x_c$ on test X can be converted to the score $y_c^*$ on test Y, and this converted cut-off score may be used to make the appropriate decision for examinees taking test Y.

### Classical Methods of Equating

Classical methods of equating were described in detail by Angoff (1971) and Kolen (1988). In general, the methods fall into the two main categories: equipercentile equating and linear equating. Equipercentile equating is accomplished by considering the scores on tests X and Y to be equivalent if their respective percentile ranks in any given group are equal. Strictly speaking, in order to equate scores on two tests, the tests must be given to the same group of examinees. In practice, the process typically is carried out by giving the tests to randomly equivalent groups of examinees.

In linear equating, it is assumed that the score $x$ on test X and the score $y$ on test Y are linearly related, that is,

$$y = ax + b$$

The coefficients $a$ and $b$ may be determined using the relationships

$$\mu_y = a\mu_x + b$$

and

$$\sigma_y = a\sigma_x$$

where $\mu_x (\mu_y)$ and $\sigma_x (\sigma_y)$ are means and standard deviations of the scores on tests X and Y, respectively. It follows that

$$a = \frac{\sigma_y}{\sigma_x} \qquad b = \mu_y - \frac{\sigma_y}{\sigma_x}\mu_x$$

and

$$y = \frac{\sigma_y}{\sigma_x}(x - \mu_x) + \mu_y.$$

Using the above expression, a score $x$ may be placed on the metric of test Y. The above expression can be obtained also by equating the standard score on text X to the standard score on test Y,

$$\frac{x - \mu_x}{\sigma_x} = \frac{y - \mu_y}{\sigma_y}$$

The assumption in linear equating is that the two test score distributions differ only with respect to their means and standard deviations. Therefore, standard scores will be equal in such cases. When this assumption is valid, linear equating becomes a special case of equipercentile equating; otherwise, it may be considered an approximation to equipercentile equating.

The linear equating method has many refinements. Procedures that take into account, for example, outliers and the unreliability of the test scores are given in Angoff (1971). Our purpose here is to describe briefly the classical equating procedures and to note the problems inherent in such approaches.

Lord (1977, 1980) has argued that in equating test scores, it should be a matter of indifference to the examinees at every given ability level whether they take test X or test Y. This notion of equity has several implications (Lord, 1977, 1980).

1. Tests measuring different traits cannot be equated.
2. Raw scores on unequally reliable tests cannot be equated (since otherwise a score from an unreliable test can be equated to the score on a reliable test, thus obviating the need for constructing reliable tests!).
3. Raw scores on tests with varying difficulty cannot be equated since the tests will not be equally reliable at different ability levels.
4. Fallible scores on tests X and Y cannot be equated unless the tests are strictly parallel.
5. Perfectly reliable tests can be equated.

In addition to the above requirements of equity, two further conditions—symmetry and invariance—must be set for equating tests. The condition of symmetry dictates that equating should not depend on which test is used as the reference test. For example, if a regression procedure is used to determine the constants in the linear equating formula, the condition of symmetry will not be met because the regression coefficients for predicting $y$ from $x$ are different from those for predicting $x$ from $y$. The requirement of invariance is that the equating procedure be sample independent.

These conditions, particularly those of equity, will usually not be met when using classical methods of equating. Theoretically, item response theory overcomes these problems. If the item response model fits the data, direct comparison of the ability parameters of two examinees who take different tests is made possible by the invariance property. Equating of test scores is obviated in an item response theory framework; what must be ensured, however, is that the item and ability parameter values based on two tests are on a common scale. Thus, in an item response theory framework, *scaling* rather than equating is necessary.

Nevertheless, because of the prevalence of the term *equating* in the literature, the terms *scaling* and *equating* will be used interchangeably in this chapter.

## Scaling or Equating in Item Response Theory

According to item response theory, the ability parameter $\theta$ of an examinee is invariant across subsets of items. This means that, apart from measurement error, ability estimates also will be invariant across subsets of items. Hence, two examinees who respond to different subsets of items (or different tests) for which the item parameter values are known will have ability estimates that are on the same scale. No equating or scaling is necessary.

When the item and ability estimates are unknown, however, the situation changes. In this case, as explained in the chapter on estimation, $\theta$ may be replaced by $\theta^* = \alpha\theta + \beta$, $b$ may be replaced by $b^* = \alpha b + \beta$, and $a$ may be replaced by $a^* = a / \alpha$ without affecting the probability of a correct response. (For the one-parameter model, since $a = 1$, $\theta$ need only be replaced by $\theta^* = \theta + \beta$, and $b$ by $b^* = b + \beta$.) This invariance of the item response function with respect to linear transformations introduces an indeterminacy in the scale that must be removed before estimation of parameters can proceed. One way to remove the indeterminacy is to fix arbitrarily the scale of $\theta$ (or $b$); in the two- and three-parameter models, the common practice is to set the mean and standard deviation of the $\theta$ (or $b$) values to be 0 and 1, respectively. For the one-parameter model, the mean of $\theta$ (or $b$) is set to 0. Fixing the scale on $\theta$ or $b$ is arbitrary and is dictated sometimes by the computer program used (in BICAL, for example, the mean of $b$ is set to 0). This scaling must be undone when attempting to compare the item parameter values or the ability parameter values across two groups.

To illustrate the procedures and principles underlying scaling, consider the situation in which one test is administered to two groups of examinees (as in studies of DIF). Suppose also that the estimation of item and ability parameters is carried out *separately* for the two groups. During the estimation phase, it is necessary to fix the scale of the parameter estimates. The two possible ways of fixing the scale are (a) standardizing the item difficulty values, that is, fixing the mean and standard deviation of the difficulty values to be 0 and 1, respectively; and (b) standardizing the ability values.

First, consider the situation in which the scaling is done on the difficulty parameters. Since the same test is administered to the two groups, the item parameter estimates must be identical (except sampling fluctuations) if the model fits the data. Hence, scaling on the difficulty values will place the item parameter estimates and the ability estimates on the same scale.

Suppose that the scaling is carried out on the ability values. Since the means and standard deviations of ability for the two groups of examinees usually will not be the same, standardizing on ability will result in item parameters that are on different scales. The item parameters will, nevertheless, be linearly related according to the linear relationship

$$b_A = \alpha b_B + \beta$$

$$a_A = \frac{a_B}{\alpha}$$

where $b_A$ and $a_A$ are the difficulty and discrimination parameter estimates in Group A, and $b_B$ and $a_B$ are the corresponding values in Group B. Once $\sigma$ and $\beta$ are determined, the item parameter estimates in Group B may be placed on the same scale as the item parameter estimates for Group A.

The more interesting problem is that of comparing the ability parameters in Group A with those in Group B. Using the same relationship as for the $b$ values above, all the ability estimates $\theta_B$ in Group B may be placed on the same scale as those in Group A, using the linear relationship

$$\theta_A^* = \alpha \theta_B + \beta$$

where $\theta_A^*$ is the value of the parameter $\theta_B$ on the scale of Group A.

The reverse situation to that described above is when one group of examinees takes two tests, X and Y. Since the ability parameter of the examinees taking the two tests must be the same, setting the mean and standard deviation of the $\theta$ to 0 and 1, respectively, places the item parameters for the two tests on a common scale. If, however, the mean and standard deviation of the difficulty parameter values for each test are set to 0 and 1, respectively, the ability parameter values in the two tests will differ by a linear transformation,

$$\theta_Y = \alpha\,\theta_X + \beta$$

The item parameters for tests X and Y must be placed on a common scale using the following relationship:

$$b_Y = \alpha\,b_X + \beta$$

$$a_Y = \frac{a_X}{\alpha}$$

These examples indicate that if it is necessary to compare examinees who take different tests, or if it is necessary to place items from different tests on a common scale, the equating study must be designed carefully. Clearly, if different groups of examinees take different tests, no comparison or equating is possible. Designs that permit "linking" of tests and comparison of examinees are discussed next.

*Linking Designs.* In many situations, the interest is in placing the item parameter estimates from two or more tests on a common scale. This placement enables comparison of the difficulty levels of the tests and also facilitates the development of item banks (see Vale, 1986). The four linking designs that permit the scaling of item parameters (or their estimates) are the following:

1. *Single-Group Design.* The two tests to be linked are given to the same group of examinees. This is a simple design, but it may be impractical to implement because testing time will be long. Moreover, practice and fatigue effects (if the two tests are administered one after the other) may have an effect on parameter estimation and, hence, on the linking results.

2. *Equivalent-Groups Design.* The two tests to be linked are given to equivalent but not identical groups of examinees, chosen randomly. This design is more practical and avoids practice and fatigue effects.

3. *Anchor-Test Design.* The tests to be linked are given to two different groups of examinees. Each test has a set of common items that may be internal or external to the tests. This design is feasible and frequently used, and, if the anchor items are chosen properly (see, for example, Klein & Jarjoura, 1985), it avoids the problems in the single-group or equivalent-groups designs.

4. *Common-Person Design.* The two tests to be linked are given to two groups of examinees, with a common group of examinees taking both tests. Because the testing will be lengthy for the common group, this design has the same drawbacks as the single-group design.

In the single-group or equivalent-groups design, where one group of examinees (or equivalent groups of examinees) takes the two tests, the methods described in the previous section may be used to place the items on the same scale. In determining the scaling constants in the equivalent-groups design, matched pairs of ability values are needed; this need presents a problem, because the groups consist of different examinees. One possible way to match examinees is to rank order the examinees in the two groups and to consider examinees with the same rank to be equivalent.

In the anchor test design, the parameters and, hence, their estimates (subject to sampling fluctuations) are related linearly in the two tests, that is,

$$b_{Yc} = \alpha \, b_{Xc} + \beta$$

$$a_{Yc} = \frac{a_{Xc}}{\alpha}$$

where $b_{Yc}$ and $b_{Xc}$ are the difficulties of the common items embedded in tests Y and X, respectively. Once the constants $\sigma$ and $\beta$ are determined, the item parameter estimates for all items in test X may be placed on the same scale as test Y. The adjusted item parameter estimates for the common items in test X will not be identical to the corresponding item parameter estimates in test Y (because of estimation errors) and, hence, they should be averaged.

Of the designs described above, the anchor test design is the most feasible. Hence, determination of the scaling constants will be discussed with reference to this design.

## Determination of the Scaling Constants

The methods available for determining the scaling constants $\alpha$ and $\beta$ (only $\beta$ when the one-parameter model is used) may be classified as follows:

1. Regression Method
2. Mean and Sigma Method
3. Robust Mean and Sigma Method
4. Characteristic Curve Method

*Regression Method.* Once pairs of values of item parameter estimates in the two groups are obtained, a regression procedure may be used to determine the line of best fit through the points,

$$b_{Yc} = \alpha b_{Xc} + \beta + e$$

The term $e$ indicates the error in fitting the line, since not all the points will be exactly on the line. Here $b_{Yc}$ and $b_{Xc}$ are the item difficulty parameter estimates for the common items in tests Y and X. If common examinees are used, the equation is

$$\theta_{Yc} = \alpha \theta_{Xc} + \beta + e$$

where $\theta_{Yc}$ and $\theta_{Xc}$ are the ability estimates for an examinee taking tests Y and X, respectively.

The estimates $\hat{\alpha}$ and $\hat{\beta}$ of the regression coefficients are

$$\hat{\alpha} = r\frac{s_{Yc}}{s_{Xc}} \qquad \text{and} \qquad \hat{\beta} = \bar{b}_{Yc} - \hat{\alpha}\bar{b}_{Xc}$$

where $r$ is the correlation coefficient between the estimates of the difficulty parameters for the common items, $\bar{b}_{Yc}$ and $\bar{b}_{Xc}$ are the respective means, and $s_{Yc}$ and $s_{Xc}$ are the respective standard deviations. In the common-examinee design, these values are replaced by corresponding values for the $\theta$ estimates.

The problem with the regression approach is that the condition of symmetry is not met. This is true because the coefficients for predicting $b_{Yc}$ from $b_{Xc}$ are different from those for predicting $b_{Xc}$ from $b_{Yc}$ and cannot be obtained by simply inverting the prediction equation

$$b_{Yc} = \hat{\alpha}b_{Xc} + \hat{\beta}$$

That is, it does not follow that

$$b_{Xc} = \frac{b_{Yc} - \hat{\beta}}{\hat{\alpha}}$$

Therefore, the regression approach is not a suitable procedure for determining the scaling constants.

*Mean and Sigma Method.* Since

$$b_{Yc} = \alpha \, b_{Xc} + \beta$$

it follows that

$$\bar{b}_{Yc} = \alpha \, \bar{b}_{Xc} + \beta$$

and

$$s_{Yc} = \alpha \, s_{Xc}$$

Thus

$$\alpha = \frac{s_{Yc}}{s_{Xc}}$$

and

$$\beta = \bar{b}_{Yc} - \alpha \, \bar{b}_{Xc}$$

Moreover, since

$$b_{Yc} = \alpha \, b_{Xc} + \beta$$

the transformation from $b_{Yc}$ to $b_{Xc}$ may be obtained as

$$b_{Xc} = \frac{b_{Yc} - \beta}{\alpha}$$

Hence, the symmetry requirement is satisfied by the mean and sigma method (when using the common-examinee design, the means and standard deviations of the corresponding $\theta$ estimates are used to determine $\alpha$ and $\beta$).

Once $\alpha$ and $\beta$ are determined, the item parameter estimates for test X are placed on the same scale as test Y using the relationships

$$b_Y^* = \alpha \, b_X + \beta$$

$$a_Y^* = \frac{a_X}{\alpha}$$

where $b_Y^*$ and $a_Y^*$ are the difficulty and discrimination values of items in test X placed on the scale of test Y. The parameter estimates of the common items are averaged, since they will not be identical, as a result of estimation errors.

For the one-parameter model, the item difficulty estimates for the common items are related as

$$b_{Yc} = b_{Xc} + \beta$$

that is, $\alpha = 1$. It follows that

$$\bar{b}_{Yc} = \bar{b}_{Xc} + \beta$$

and, hence,

$$\beta = \bar{b}_{Yc} - \bar{b}_{Xc}$$

Thus, the item difficulty estimates for test X are transformed by adding the difference in the mean difficulty levels of the common items.

*Robust Mean and Sigma Method.* In the mean and sigma method described above, no consideration was given to the fact that item parameters are estimated with varying degrees of accuracy (i.e., some difficulty estimates have larger standard errors than others). Linn et al. (1981) proposed the robust mean and sigma method to take into account the fact that the parameter estimates have different standard errors. Each pair of values ($b_{Yci}$, $b_{Xci}$) for common item $i$ in tests Y and X is weighted by the inverse of the larger of the variances of the two estimates. Pairs with large variances receive low weights, and pairs with small variances receive high weights. The variance of the difficulty parameter estimate is obtained by first inverting the information matrix (see chapter 3) and taking the appropriate diagonal element. For the three-parameter model the information matrix is of dimension $3 \times 3$, while for the one-parameter model it is of dimension $1 \times 1$; that is, it has a single element.

The steps in carrying out the robust mean and sigma method are summarized below:

1. For each pair $(b_{Yci}, b_{Xci})$, determine the weight, $w_i$ as

$$w_i = [\,\text{maximum}\,\{\,v(b_{Yci}),\,v(b_{Xci})\,\}\,]^{-1}$$

   where $v(b_{Yci})$ and $v(b_{Xci})$ are the variances of the estimates of the common items.

2. Scale the weights:

$$w'_i = w_i \,/\, \sum_{j=1}^{k} w_j$$

   where $k$ is the number of common items in tests X and Y.

3. Compute the weighted estimates:

$$b'_{Yci} = w'_i\, b_{Yci}$$

$$b'_{Xci} = w'_i\, b_{Xci}$$

4. Determine the means and standard deviations of the weighted item parameter estimates.

5. Determine $\alpha$ and $\beta$ using the means and standard deviations of the weighted estimates.

Stocking and Lord (1983) have suggested that further improvement in determining $\alpha$ and $\beta$ may be obtained if outliers are taken into account in the computation of the mean and standard deviation. The weights are made more robust by basing them on the perpendicular distances of points from the line

$$b_{Yc} = \alpha b_{Xc} + \beta$$

Starting with an initial value for $\alpha$ and $\beta$, the process is repeated until the $\alpha$ and $\beta$ values do not change. For details of this procedure, refer to Stocking and Lord (1983) or Hambleton and Swaminathan (1985).

*Characteristic Curve Method.* The mean and sigma method (and its robust version) capitalizes on the relationship that exists between the difficulty parameters and ignores the relationship that exists between the discrimination parameters in determining the scaling constants. Haebara (1980) and Stocking and Lord (1983) have proposed the "characteristic curve" method, which takes into account the information available from both the item difficulty and item discrimination parameters.

The true score $\tau_{Xa}$ of an examinee with ability $\theta_a$ on the $k$ common items in test X is

$$\tau_{Xa} = \sum_{i=1}^{k} P(\theta_a, b_{Xci}, a_{Xci}, c_{Xci})$$

Similarly, the true score $\tau_{Ya}$ of an examinee with the same ability $\theta_a$ on the $k$ common items in test Y is

$$\tau_{Ya} = \sum_{j=1}^{k} P(\theta_a, b_{Yci}, a_{Yci}, c_{Yci})$$

For the set of common items,

$$b_{Yci} = \alpha \, b_{Xci} + \beta$$

$$a_{Yci} = \frac{a_{Xci}}{\alpha}$$

and

$$c_{Yci} = c_{Xci}$$

The constants $\alpha$ and $\beta$ are chosen to minimize the function $F$ where

$$F = \frac{1}{N} \sum_{a=1}^{N} (\tau_{Xa} - \tau_{Ya})^2$$

and $N$ is the number of examinees. The function $F$ is a function of $\alpha$ and $\beta$ and is an indication of the discrepancy between $\tau_{Xa}$ and $\tau_{Ya}$. The procedure for determining $\alpha$ and $\beta$ is iterative, and details are provided in Stocking and Lord (1983).

In using the anchor test design, the number of anchor items and, more important, their characteristics play a key role in the quality of the linking. For example, if the anchor items are too easy for one group and too difficult for the other, the parameter estimates obtained in the two groups will be unstable, and the linking will be poor. It is important, therefore, that the common items be in an acceptable range of difficulty for the two groups. Empirical evidence suggests that best results are obtained if the common items are representative of the content of the two tests to be linked. In addition, it is important to ensure that the two groups of examinees are reasonably similar in their ability distributions, at least with respect to the common items. A rule of thumb for the number of anchor items is that the number should be approximately 20% to 25% of the number of items in the tests.

## Other Linking and Equating Procedures

With the anchor test design, concurrent calibration using the LOGIST computer program permits placing the item parameter estimates and ability parameter estimates on a common scale without the need for a separate linking and scaling step. (A similar analysis with the one-parameter model can be carried out with the RIDA computer program.) The procedure is as follows:

1. Treat the data as if $(N_X + N_Y)$ examinees have taken a test with $(n_X + n_Y + n_a)$ items where $n_a$ denotes the number of anchor items.
2. Treat the $n_Y$ items to which the $N_X$ examinees did not respond as "not reached" items and code them as such. Similarly, code the $n_X$ items to which the $N_Y$ examinees did not respond as "not reached."
3. Estimate the item and ability parameters.

This procedure is simple to implement. Currently, little information exists regarding the accuracy of this procedure; further investigation of this issue is needed.

In addition to the "linking" procedures described above, item response theory methods may be used to (a) equate true scores on two tests, and (b) equate two tests using "observed score" distributions generated for given levels of θ. These procedures are described in Lord (1980) and Hambleton and Swaminathan (1985). The reader is referred to these sources for more details.

The steps in carrying out a linking are illustrated using two examples. In the first example, the linking procedure is illustrated in the context of developing an item bank. The second example deals with the problem of linking two tests. In both examples, the linking is carried out using an anchor test design.

## Example 1

Assume that a bank of test items that have been calibrated using the one-parameter model is available. The item difficulty estimates for the item bank are given in the Appendix. It is desirable to add to the existing bank a set of 15 new, uncalibrated items. To add these 15 items to the existing bank, we could use the anchor test design with five anchor items chosen from the existing bank. Suppose that the $b$ values for these five items are 1.65, 1.20, −0.80, −1.25, and 2.50. These anchor items were chosen carefully to match the content and, it was hoped, the difficulty levels of the 15 experimental items. Since the 15 items are untested, however, it is difficult to assess their difficulty levels a priori. This information could be obtained from a pilot test.

In determining the scaling constants, the mean and sigma method is used for illustrative purposes because of its simplicity. The steps are as follows:

1. The 20-item test (15 experimental and 5 anchor items) is administered to an appropriate sample of examinees (200 in this example).
2. An appropriate IRT model is chosen—this must be the same as the model on which the existing item bank is used. Since, for illustration, we have assumed that the items in the bank fit a one-parameter model, a one-parameter model is fitted also to the 20-item test (with appropriate checks on model-data fit).
3. The mean difficulty level of the five anchor items $\bar{b}_{Yc}$ (from the item bank, designated as test Y) based on their known item parameter values is computed; the mean value is 0.66.

4. The 20-item test is calibrated, using (say) the computer program BICAL. The mean of the difficulties based on the 20-item test will be set to zero in the estimation process. The mean of the five anchor items that is part of the 20-item test is computed and designated as $\bar{b}_{Xc}$, with a computed value of 0.25.

5. Since the item difficulties of the common items are related linearly according to

$$b_{Yc} = b_{Xc} + \beta$$

Beta is calculated as $\bar{b}_{Yc} - \bar{b}_{Xc}$. (Note that $\alpha = 1$ because the model used is the one-parameter model.) In this example, $\beta = 0.66 - 0.25 = 0.41$.

6. The item difficulty estimates of the 15 experimental items are adjusted by adding $(\bar{b}_{Yc} - \bar{b}_{Xc}) = 0.41$ to each difficulty estimate.

7. The common items that are part of the experimental set are adjusted by adding $(\bar{b}_{Yc} - \bar{b}_{Xc})$ to each item difficulty value. Since the adjusted values will be different from the values for the common items in the item bank, the adjusted difficulty values are averaged with the difficulty values for the common items in the item bank.

8. The 15 experimental items are on the same scale as the items in the item bank and are added to the item bank. The estimates for the common items are revised.

These calculations are summarized in Table 9.1. The new items and their difficulty values have been added to the item bank (items 76 to 90) reported in the Appendix.

## Example 2

In this example, two proficiency tests, each with 15 items, were administered to samples of New Mexico high school students during two consecutive spring terms. Unfortunately, none of the test items came from the item bank in the Appendix, and, therefore, parameter estimates for all of the test items had to be obtained. It was desired to place the items in the test that was administered first on the same scale as the items in the test administered second. Hence, the test administered first is labeled as test X and the second as test Y.

An anchor test design was used for the linking. The anchor test, with six items, was constructed to be representative in content of both test X

**TABLE 9.1** Linking Procedure for Placing Experimental Items (Text X) on the Same Scale as Items in an Item Bank (Test Y)[a]

| Item | Test X Difficulty $b_X$ | Test Y Difficulty Common Items $b_{Yc}$ | Scaled Test X Difficulty $b_X + (\bar{b}_{Yc} - \bar{b}_{Xc})$ | Scaled Test X Difficulty (Revised)[b] |
|---|---|---|---|---|
| 1 | **1.29** | **1.65** | **1.70** | 1.67 |
| 2 | **0.75** | **1.20** | **1.16** | 1.18 |
| 3 | **−1.24** | **−0.80** | **−0.83** | −0.82 |
| 4 | **−1.72** | **−1.25** | **−1.31** | −1.28 |
| 5 | **2.17** | **2.50** | **2.58** | 2.54 |
| 6 | 0.85 | | 1.26 | 1.26 |
| 7 | −1.88 | | −1.47 | −1.47 |
| 8 | −2.02 | | −1.61 | −1.61 |
| 9 | 0.19 | | 0.60 | 0.60 |
| 10 | 0.22 | | 0.63 | 0.63 |
| 11 | −1.86 | | −1.45 | −1.45 |
| 12 | −1.32 | | −0.91 | −0.91 |
| 13 | −1.10 | | −0.69 | −0.69 |
| 14 | 0.74 | | 1.15 | 1.15 |
| 15 | 0.61 | | 1.02 | 1.02 |
| 16 | 0.50 | | 0.91 | 0.91 |
| 17 | −0.80 | | −0.39 | −0.39 |
| 18 | 1.70 | | 2.11 | 2.11 |
| 19 | 1.37 | | 1.78 | 1.78 |
| 20 | 1.55 | | 1.96 | 1.96 |

$$\bar{b}_{Xc} = 0.25 \qquad \bar{b}_{Yc} = 0.66 \qquad \bar{b}_{Yc} - \bar{b}_{Xc} = 0.41$$

a. Common items are in bold.
b. Common item difficulties for tests X and Y have been averaged.

and test Y. The tests were administered to 500 examinees on each occasion.

In choosing an item response model, based on pilot studies, it was decided to use a three-parameter model with a fixed $c$ value of 0.2. The item and ability parameters were estimated using the LOGIST computer program; in the estimation phase, the mean and standard deviation of $\theta$ were set to be 0 and 1, respectively.

In carrying out the linking, the mean and sigma method was used, primarily for pedagogical purposes. The robust mean and sigma or the characteristic curve methods are more appropriate but are not used here because of the nature of the computations involved.

The steps in carrying out the linking are as follows:

1. Compute the mean and standard deviation of the difficulty estimates for the common items embedded in tests X and Y.
2. Determine the constants $\alpha$ and $\beta$ (since the three-parameter model was used).
3. Scale the difficulty estimates for test X by multiplying them by $\alpha$ and adding $\beta$.
4. Average the difficulty values for the common items.
5. Scale the discrimination parameter estimates for test X by dividing them by $\alpha$.
6. Average the discrimination parameter values for the common items.

The difficulty and discrimination parameter estimates for test X are now on the same scale as those in test Y. The calculations are summarized in Tables 9.2 and 9.3.

The constants $\alpha$ and $\beta$ can be used to place the ability values of the examinees taking tests X and Y on a common scale. Since

$$\theta_Y = \alpha\,\theta_X + \beta = 0.95\,\theta_X - 0.18,$$

the mean ability of the examinees who took test X may be converted to a mean on test Y, had they taken it, enabling a comparison of the mean abilities of the two groups even though they took different tests. For the group who took test X, the mean $\theta$ value was set to zero in the estimation phase. Converting this mean to a mean on the scale of test Y, we obtain

$$\overline{\theta}_Y = 0.95(0) - 0.18 = -0.18$$

This implies that the difference in the mean abilities for the two groups taking tests X and Y is $-0.18$; the group taking test X had a lower mean ability than the group taking test Y. This information could be used for academic or program evaluation purposes.

**TABLE 9.2** Determination of Scaling Constants and Scaled Difficulty for Tests X and Y[a]

| Item | Test Y Difficulty | Test X Difficulty | Scaled Difficulty All Items[b] |
|---|---|---|---|
| 1 | 1.20 | | 1.20 |
| 2 | 1.75 | | 1.75 |
| 3 | −0.80 | | −0.80 |
| 4 | −1.28 | | −1.28 |
| 5 | 1.35 | | 1.35 |
| 6 | 1.40 | | 1.40 |
| 7 | 1.20 | | 1.20 |
| 8 | 0.50 | | 0.50 |
| 9 | 0.72 | | 0.72 |
| 10 | −1.95 | | −1.95 |
| 11 | −2.20 | | −2.20 |
| 12 | 2.40 | | 2.40 |
| 13 | 1.80 | | 1.80 |
| 14 | 1.45 | | 1.45 |
| 15 | 0.80 | | 0.80 |
| 16 | **1.10** | **1.20** | 1.03 |
| 17 | **1.85** | **2.10** | 1.83 |
| 18 | **2.30** | **2.75** | 2.36 |
| 19 | **−1.50** | **−1.40** | −1.51 |
| 20 | **−1.80** | **−1.65** | −1.78 |
| 21 | **0.40** | **0.60** | 0.40 |
| 22 | | 1.81 | 1.54 |
| 23 | | 2.20 | 1.91 |
| 24 | | 2.70 | 2.38 |
| 25 | | 1.86 | 1.59 |
| 26 | | −0.90 | −1.04 |
| 27 | | −1.10 | −1.23 |
| 28 | | −2.30 | −2.37 |
| 29 | | 0.58 | 0.37 |
| 30 | | 0.92 | 0.69 |
| 31 | | 0.88 | 0.66 |
| 32 | | 1.92 | 1.64 |
| 33 | | 2.10 | 1.82 |
| 34 | | 2.52 | 2.21 |
| 35 | | 1.60 | 1.34 |
| 36 | | −1.20 | −1.32 |

| | | |
|---|---|---|
| $\bar{b}_{Yc} = 0.39$ | $\bar{b}_{Xc} = 0.60$ | $\alpha = 0.95$ |
| $S_{Yc} = 1.56$ | $S_{Xc} = 1.65$ | $\beta = -0.18$ |

a. Common items are in bold.
b. Common items are averaged; scaled difficulty values for test X = $\alpha b_X + \beta$.

**TABLE 9.3** Discrimination Values for Tests X and Y[a]

| Item | Test Y Discrimination | Test X Discrimination | Scaled Discrimination All Items[b] |
|------|------|------|------|
| 1 | 1.02 | | 1.02 |
| 2 | 1.21 | | 1.21 |
| 3 | 0.90 | | 0.90 |
| 4 | 0.72 | | 0.72 |
| 5 | 1.25 | | 1.25 |
| 6 | 1.40 | | 1.40 |
| 7 | 1.12 | | 1.12 |
| 8 | 0.75 | | 0.75 |
| 9 | 0.92 | | 0.92 |
| 10 | 0.62 | | 0.62 |
| 11 | 0.52 | | 0.52 |
| 12 | 1.98 | | 1.98 |
| 13 | 1.90 | | 1.90 |
| 14 | 1.62 | | 1.62 |
| 15 | 1.01 | | 1.01 |
| 16 | **0.95** | **0.90** | 0.95 |
| 17 | **1.23** | **1.15** | 1.22 |
| 18 | **2.00** | **1.86** | 1.98 |
| 19 | **0.68** | **0.55** | 0.63 |
| 20 | **0.45** | **0.40** | 0.44 |
| 21 | **0.70** | **0.65** | 0.69 |
| 22 | | 1.60 | 1.68 |
| 23 | | 1.85 | 1.95 |
| 24 | | 1.90 | 2.00 |
| 25 | | 1.62 | 1.70 |
| 26 | | 0.81 | 0.85 |
| 27 | | 0.62 | 0.65 |
| 28 | | 0.40 | 0.42 |
| 29 | | 0.64 | 0.67 |
| 30 | | 0.80 | 0.84 |
| 31 | | 0.75 | 0.79 |
| 32 | | 1.23 | 1.29 |
| 33 | | 1.55 | 1.63 |
| 34 | | 1.72 | 1.81 |
| 35 | | 1.12 | 1.18 |
| 36 | | 0.42 | 0.44 |
| | | | $\alpha = 0.95$ |

a. Common items are in bold.
b. Common items are averaged; scaled discrimination values for test X = $\alpha a_X$.

## Summary

Classical methods for equating have several shortcomings; most important, the condition of equity usually will not be met when using classical methods. Item response theory methods obviate the need for equating because of the property of invariance of item and ability parameters. Because of the scaling that is needed to eliminate the indeterminacy in item response models, item and ability parameters will be invariant only up to a linear transformation; that is, the item and ability parameters of the same items and same examinees will be related linearly in two groups. Once the linear relationship is identified, item parameter estimates and ability parameter estimates may be placed on a common scale. This procedure, known as linking or scaling, may be completed using several designs. The most important design is the anchor test design, where two tests containing a common set of items are administered to two different groups of examinees. Using the common items and one of several methods, the coefficients of the linear transformation relating the item parameters for the two tests can be determined. With knowledge of the linear transformation, the item and ability parameter estimates may be placed on a common scale. An excellent review of various designs for linking items to a common scale is provided by Vale (1986).

## Exercises for Chapter 9

1. In DIF studies, the same test is administered to two different groups and the item parameters are estimated separately. Before comparing the item parameters for the two groups, they must be placed on the same scale. Explain how you would ensure that the item parameters are on a common scale.

2. Suppose that in an equating study two different tests are given to two different groups of examinees, with a common subset of examinees taking both tests. Explain the procedure you would use to place the item and ability parameter estimates for the two tests and the two groups on the same scale.

3. In Example 1 of chapter 9, it was assumed that the one-parameter model fitted the data.

   a. Determine the scaling constants for placing the experimental items on the same scale as the items in the bank, assuming that a two-parameter model fits the data.

b. Place the *b* values of the common items in the experimental test on the same scale as the *b* values of the common items in the bank.

c. How similar are the difficulty values of the common items for the one- and two-parameter models? Carry out this comparison by plotting the scaled difficulty values for the one- and two-parameter models against the "true" item bank values.

4. Two tests, A and B, with 10 common items were administered to two groups of examinees, and a three-parameter model was fitted to the data. The means and standard deviations for the *b* values of the common items are given in Table 9.4.

**TABLE 9.4**

|        | Test A | Test B |
|--------|--------|--------|
| Mean   | 3.5    | 4.2    |
| SD     | 1.8    | 2.2    |

The difficulty and discrimination values for an item in test B are –1.4 and 0.9, respectively. Place these values on the same scale as test A.

## Answers to Exercises for Chapter 9

1. Standardize the item difficulty parameter estimates.

2. Since a common set of examinees have taken both tests, their abilities must be the same. Because of standardization during the estimation phase, however, the $\theta$ values will be related linearly according to

$$\theta_{Xc} = \alpha\,\theta_{Yc} + \beta$$

The means and SDs of the common $\theta$ values are used to determine $\alpha$ and $\beta$, as indicated for the anchor item equating procedure. With the relationship established, the abilities of examinees taking test Y and the item difficulties for test Y can be mapped onto the scale defined for test X. The item discrimination indices for test Y are mapped onto the test X scale using the transformation

$$a_X = \frac{a_Y}{\alpha}$$

3.  a. $\alpha = 0.97$, $\beta = 0.42$.
    b. See Table 9.5.

**TABLE 9.5**

|                              | Common Items | | | | |
|                              | 1    | 2    | 3     | 4     | 5    |
|------------------------------|------|------|-------|-------|------|
| Scaled common items (2P):    | 1.67 | 1.15 | −0.78 | −1.25 | 2.52 |
| Scaled common items (1P):    | 1.70 | 1.16 | −0.83 | −1.31 | 2.58 |
| Common items from bank:      | 1.65 | 1.20 | −0.80 | −1.25 | 2.50 |

  c. The estimates of item difficulty for the one- and two-parameter models are fairly similar, but the estimates for the two-parameter model are closer to the values in the bank.

4.  The scaling constants for placing items in test B on the same scale as test A (let X = test B and Y = test A) are $\alpha = 0.82$ and $\beta = 0.06$. The scaled item difficulty values are −1.09 and 1.10.

# 10

## Computerized Adaptive Testing

### Background

In previous chapters, it was shown that a test provides the most precise measurement of an examinee's ability when the difficulty of the test is matched to the ability level of the examinee. Any single test administered to a group of examinees cannot provide the same precision of measurement for every examinee. The ideal testing situation would be to give every examinee a test that is "tailored," or adapted, to the examinee's ability level.

The earliest application of tailored or adaptive testing was in the work of Binet on intelligence testing in 1908 (Weiss, 1985). Little additional work on adaptive testing took place, however, until Fred Lord at the Educational Testing Service began a comprehensive research program in the late 1960s (for a review of his work, see Lord, 1980). Lord pursued adaptive testing because he felt fixed-length tests were inefficient for most examinees, but especially for low- and high-ability examinees. Lord felt that tests could be shortened without any loss of measurement precision if the test items administered to each examinee were chosen so as to provide maximum information about the examinee's ability. In theory, each examinee would be administered a unique set of items.

Adaptive testing became feasible only with the advent of computers. The computer's immense power to store test information (e.g., test items and their indices) and for producing, administering, and scoring tests has enabled the potential of adaptive testing to be fully realized (Bunderson, Inouye, & Olsen, 1989; Wainer, 1990). Since the late 1960s a substantial amount of research has been supported by the U.S. Armed Services, the U.S. Office of Personnel Management, and other federal agencies; special conferences have been held, and hundreds of papers on adaptive testing have been published (see, for example, Wainer, 1990; Weiss, 1983).

In computerized adaptive testing (CAT), the sequence of items administered to an examinee depends on the examinee's performance on earlier items in the test. Based on the examinee's prior performance, items that are maximally informative about the examinee's ability level are administered. In this way, tests may be shortened without any loss of measurement precision. High-ability examinees do not need to be administered relatively easy items, and low-ability examinees do not need to be administered the most difficult items, because such items provide little or no information about the examinee's ability.

After an examinee responds to a set of test items (sometimes only two or three items) presented at a computer terminal, an initial ability estimate for the examinee is obtained. The computer is programmed to select the next set of administered items from the available item bank that will contribute the most information about the examinee's ability, based on the initial estimate. Details of how test items are selected and ability estimates are obtained are provided in the following sections. The administration of items to the examinee continues until some specified number of items is administered or a desired level of measurement precision (i.e., standard error) of the ability estimate is attained.

## Promise of IRT

Item response models are particularly suitable for adaptive testing because it is possible to obtain ability estimates that are independent of the particular set of test items administered. In fact, adaptive testing would not be feasible without item response theory. Even though each examinee receives a different set of items, differing in difficulty, item response theory provides a framework for comparing the ability estimates of different examinees.

In applying item response theory to measurement problems, as was mentioned in chapter 2, a common assumption is that one dominant factor or ability accounts for item performance. This assumption is made, for example, in nearly all of the current applications of adaptive testing. The IRT model most appropriate in adaptive testing is the three-parameter logistic model (Green, Bock, Humphreys, Linn, & Reckase, 1984; Lord, 1980; Weiss, 1983). The main reason for choosing the three-parameter model is that it generally fits multiple-choice item data better than the one- or two-parameter models.

The item information function plays a critical role in adaptive testing. Items that contribute maximally to the precision of measurement (see chapters 6 and 7) are selected for administration. Items providing the most information are, in general, items on which the examinee has an (approximately) 50% to 60% chance of answering correctly.

## Basic Approach

In adaptive testing within an IRT framework, an attempt is made to match the difficulties of test items to the ability level of the examinee being measured. To match test items to ability levels requires a large pool of items whose statistical characteristics are known, so that suitable items may be drawn (Millman & Arter, 1984). According to Lord (1980), the computer must be programmed to accomplish the following in order to tailor a test to an examinee.

1. Predict from the examinee's previous responses how the examinee would respond to various test items not yet administered.
2. Make effective use of this knowledge to select the test item to be administered next.
3. Assign at the end of testing a numerical score that represents the ability of the examinee tested.

The advantages of computerized adaptive testing, in addition to shortening tests without loss of measurement precision, are numerous. Some of these advantages are

- enhanced test security
- testing on demand
- no need for answer sheets
- test pace that is keyed to the individual
- immediate test scoring and reporting
- the minimization of test frustration for some examinees
- greater test standardization
- easy removal of "defective items" from the item bank when they are identified

- greater flexibility in the choice of item formats
- reduction in test supervision time

Adaptive testing research to date has been focused in six areas: choice of IRT model, item bank, starting point for testing, selection of subsequent test items, scoring/ability estimation, and choice of method for deciding when to terminate the test administration. Refer to Hambleton, Zaal, and Pieters (1991) for a discussion of research in these six areas. A brief discussion of two of these—item selection and ability estimation—follows.

Two procedures are used currently for item selection in an adaptive mode (Kingsbury & Zara, 1989). The first, *maximum information* (Weiss, 1982), involves the selection of an item that provides maximum information (i.e., minimizes the standard error) at the examinee's ability level. To avoid the same items being selected time and time again (items with the highest levels of discriminating power, in general, provide the most information) and thereby (possibly) affecting test security and, subsequently, test validity, Green et al. (1984) have suggested that items be selected on a random basis from among items that provide the greatest information at the ability level of interest. Thus, for practical reasons, slightly less than optimal items usually are administered to examinees.

The second method, *Bayesian item selection* (Owen, 1975), involves the selection of the test item that minimizes the variance of the posterior distribution of the examinee's ability (see chapter 3). As more test items are administered, the posterior distribution becomes more concentrated, reflecting the precision with which the examinee's ability is estimated. Bayesian methods require specification of a prior belief about the examinee's ability; hence, the success of the method depends in part on the appropriateness of the prior distribution. The impact of the prior distribution diminishes as more items are administered.

An important advantage of computerized adaptive testing is that test scoring/ability estimation is carried out while the test is being administered; thus, feedback of results to examinees may be provided at the completion of testing. In obtaining ability estimates, the two estimation procedures commonly used are maximum likelihood and Bayesian (see Weiss, 1982, and chapter 3, this volume). Maximum likelihood estimation poses problems when the number of test items is small. Bayesian procedures overcome the problems encountered with maximum likelihood procedures but may produce biased estimates of ability if inappropriate prior distributions are chosen.

## Example

This example, which highlights the features of CAT ability estimation and item selection, was prepared by Reshetar (1990). For the purposes of the example, Reshetar created a bank of 13 test items, contained in Table 10.1.

**TABLE 10.1**

| | Item Parameter | | |
|---|---|---|---|
| *Item* | *b* | *a* | *c* |
| 1 | 0.09 | 1.11 | 0.22 |
| 2 | 0.47 | 1.21 | 0.24 |
| 3 | −0.55 | 1.78 | 0.22 |
| 4 | 1.01 | 1.39 | 0.08 |
| 5 | −1.88 | 1.22 | 0.07 |
| 6 | −0.82 | 1.52 | 0.09 |
| 7 | 1.77 | 1.49 | 0.02 |
| 8 | 1.92 | 0.71 | 0.19 |
| 9 | 0.69 | 1.41 | 0.13 |
| 10 | −0.28 | 0.98 | 0.01 |
| 11 | 1.47 | 1.59 | 0.04 |
| 12 | 0.23 | 0.72 | 0.02 |
| 13 | 1.21 | 0.58 | 0.17 |

Source: From *Computer Adaptive Testing: Development and Application* (p. 9) by R. Reshetar, 1990. Amherst: University of Massachusetts, School of Education.

In practice, an item bank would consist of hundreds, and possibly thousands, of test items.

A sequence of events that might occur in computerized adaptive testing is as follows:

1. Item 3 is selected; this item is of average difficulty and high discrimination. Suppose the examinee answers Item 3 correctly. A maximum likelihood estimate of ability cannot be obtained until the examinee has answered at least one item correctly and one item incorrectly. (Zero or perfect scores correspond to $-\infty$ and $+\infty$ ability estimates, respectively.)

**TABLE 10.2** Maximum-Likelihood Ability Estimates and Standard Error for One Examinee at the End of Each CAT Stage

| Stage | Item Number | Item Response | $\hat{\theta}$ | $I(\hat{\theta})$ | $SE(\hat{\theta})$[a] |
|-------|-------------|---------------|----------------|-------------------|-----------------------|
| 1     | 3           | 1             | —              | —                 | —                     |
| 2     | 12          | 1             | —              | —                 | —                     |
| 3     | 7           | 0             | 1.03           | 0.97              | 1.02                  |
| 4     | 4           | 1             | 1.46           | 2.35              | 0.65                  |
| 5     | 11          | 0             | 1.13           | 3.55              | 0.55                  |
| 6     | 9           | 1             | 1.24           | 4.61              | 0.47                  |
| 7     | 2           | 1             | 1.29           | 5.05              | 0.45                  |
| 8     | 1           | 1             | 1.31           | 5.27              | 0.44                  |
| 9     | 8           | 0             | 1.25           | 5.47              | 0.43                  |

a. $SE(\hat{\theta}) = 1 / \sqrt{I(\hat{\theta})}$

2. Another item is selected. Item 12 is chosen because it is more difficult than the previously administered item. Suppose the examinee correctly answers Item 12. Again, a maximum likelihood estimate of ability cannot be obtained.

3. Item 7 is chosen next; it is more difficult than Items 3 and 12. Suppose the examinee answers this item incorrectly. The examinee's item response vector for the three items may be represented as (1, 1, 0). Through use of the maximum likelihood procedure for estimating ability with known item parameters, an ability estimate can be obtained ($\hat{\theta} = 1.03$). The test information for the three items at this ability level is $I(\hat{\theta} = 1.03) = 0.97$, and the corresponding standard error is $SE(\hat{\theta}) = 1.02$. These values appear in Table 10.2.

4. Next, the information provided by each of the remaining items in the bank is computed at $\theta = 1.03$. These values are reported in Table 10.3. Item 4 is selected next because it provides the most information at $\theta = 1.03$. Suppose that Item 4 is administered and then is answered correctly by the examinee. A new ability estimate is obtained for the response pattern (1, 1, 0, 1). The new ability estimate is $\hat{\theta} = 1.46$.

5. The item information at $\theta = 1.46$ for the remaining items is computed. The process described above for administering an item, estimating ability, determining the information provided by unadministered items, and choosing an item to be administered next based on the information it provides is continued. To continue this procedure, Item 11 is chosen next, following by Item 9, then by Items 2, 1, and finally, 8. The procedure stops when the standard error of the examinee's ability estimate stops decreasing

**TABLE 10.3** Information Provided by Unadministered Items at Each CAT Stage

| Stage | $\hat{\theta}$ | Information Provided by Item | | | | | | | | | | | | |
| --- | --- | --- | --- | --- | --- | --- | --- | --- | --- | --- | --- | --- | --- | --- |
| | | 1 | 2 | 3 | 4 | 5 | 6 | 7 | 8 | 9 | 10 | 11 | 12 | 13 |
| 4 | 1.03 | 0.034 | 0.547 | — | 1.192 | 0.010 | 0.051 | — | 0.143 | 1.008 | 0.251 | 1.101 | — | 0.166 |
| 5 | 1.46 | 0.179 | 0.319 | — | — | 0.004 | 0.017 | — | 0.205 | 0.579 | 0.136 | 1.683 | — | 0.175 |
| 6 | 1.13 | 0.292 | 0.494 | — | — | 0.008 | 0.039 | — | 0.159 | 0.917 | 0.219 | — | — | 0.170 |
| 7 | 1.24 | 0.249 | 0.433 | — | — | 0.006 | 0.029 | — | 0.175 | — | 0.187 | — | — | 0.173 |
| 8 | 1.29 | 0.232 | — | — | — | 0.006 | 0.026 | — | 0.182 | — | 0.175 | — | — | 0.174 |
| 9 | 1.31 | — | — | — | — | 0.005 | 0.024 | — | 0.186 | — | 0.168 | — | — | 0.174 |
| 10 | 1.25 | — | — | — | — | 0.006 | 0.028 | — | — | — | 0.184 | — | — | 0.173 |

by a specified amount. As can be seen from Table 10.2, the decrease in the standard error when Item 8 is administered in stage 9 compared with the standard error at stage 8 is 0.01. The procedure stops at this point. The estimate of the examinee's ability is taken as $\hat{\theta} = 1.25$.

Weiss and Kingsbury (1984) described several other examples of application of CAT to educational testing problems.

## Exercise for Chapter 10

For the example in the chapter, suppose that an examinee was administered Items 3, 12, and 7 and responded (1, 1, 0). Item 4 was chosen to be administered next, and the examinee answered it incorrectly. The maximum likelihood estimate of ability was computed to be 0.45. Compute the information function for the remaining items at this $\theta$ value. Which item should be administered to the examinee next?

## Answer to Exercise for Chapter 10

The item information values at $\theta = 0.45$ are given in Table 10.4.

**TABLE 10.4**

| Item | 1 | 2 | 5 | 6 | 8 | 9 | 10 | 11 | 13 |
|------|------|------|------|------|------|------|------|------|------|
| Information | 0.50 | 0.66 | 0.03 | 0.19 | 0.18 | 1.06 | 0.48 | 0.45 | 0.16 |

Item 9 has the highest information at $\theta = 0.45$. It is administered next.

# 11

---

# Future Directions of Item Response Theory

We hope that Dr. Testmaker and other applied measurement specialists will find the contents of this book helpful. Many important concepts, models, features, and applications were introduced, and many examples were provided; this material should prepare our readers for the next steps in the learning process. No book, by itself, can prepare measurement specialists to use IRT models successfully in their work. Applied work with various data sets and IRT computer programs is an essential component of training in IRT. The practitioner must be ready to handle the many problems that arise in practice.

Although IRT provides solutions to many testing problems that previously were unsolved, it is not a magic wand that can be waved to overcome such deficiencies as poorly written test items and poor test designs. In the hands of careful test developers, however, IRT models and methods can become powerful tools in the design and construction of sound educational and psychological instruments, and in reporting and interpreting test results.

Research on IRT models and their applications is being conducted at a phenomenal rate (see Thissen & Steinberg, 1986, for a taxonomy of models). Entire issues of several journals have been devoted to developments in IRT. For the future, two directions for research appear to be especially important: polytomous unidimensional response models and both dichotomous and polytomous multidimensional response models. Research in both directions is well underway (Bock, 1972; Masters & Wright, 1984; Samejima, 1969, 1972, 1973, 1974). With the growing interest in "authentic measurement," special attention must be given to IRT models that can handle polytomous scoring, since authentic measurement is linked to performance testing and to nondichotomous scoring of examinee performance.

Multidimensional IRT models were introduced originally by Lord and Novick (1968) and Samejima (1974) and, more recently, by Embretson (1984) and McDonald (1989). Multidimensional models offer the prospect of better fitting current test data and providing multidimensional representations of both items and examinee abilities. It remains to be seen whether parameters for these multidimensional models can be estimated properly and whether multidimensional representations of items and examinees are useful to practitioners.

Goldstein and Wood (1989) have argued for more IRT model building in the future but feel that more attention should be given to placing IRT models within an explicit linear modeling framework. Advantages, according to Goldstein and Wood, include model parameters that are simpler to understand, easier to estimate, and that have well-known statistical properties.

In addition to the important IRT applications addressed in earlier chapters, three others are likely to draw special attention from educators and psychologists in the coming years. First, large-scale state, national, and international assessments are attracting considerable attention and will continue to do so for the foreseeable future. Item response models are being used at the all-important reporting stages in these assessments. It will be interesting to see what technical controversies arise from this type of application. One feature that plays an important role in reporting is the ICC. Are ICCs invariant to the nature and amounts of instruction? The assumption is that ICCs *are* invariant, but substantially more research is needed to establish this point.

Second, cognitive psychologists such as Embretson (1984) are interested in using IRT models to link examinees' task performances to their abilities through complex models that attempt to estimate parameters for the cognitive components needed to complete the tasks. This line of research is also consistent with Goldstein and Wood's (1989) goal of seeking more meaningful psychological models that help explain examinee test performance. Much of the IRT research to date has emphasized the use of mathematical models that provide little in the way of psychological interpretations of examinee item and test performance.

Third, educators and psychologists are making the argument for using test scores to do more than simply rank order examinees on their abilities or determine whether they have met a particular achievement level or standard. Diagnostic information is becoming increasingly important to users of test scores. *Inappropriateness measurement* developed by M. Levine and F. Drasgow (see, for example, Drasgow et al., 1987), which incorporates IRT models, provides a framework for identifying aberrant responses of examinees and special groups of examinees on individual items and groups of items. Such information may be helpful in successful diagnostic work. Greater use of IRT models in providing diagnostic information is anticipated in the coming years.

# Appendix A

# Classical and IRT Parameter Estimates
# for the New Mexico State Proficiency Exam

**TABLE A.1** Classical and IRT Item Parameter Estimates for the One-, Two-, and Three-Parameter Models

| Item | Classical | | 1P | 2P | | 3P | | |
|------|-----------|----------|--------|--------|------|--------|------|------|
| | *p* | *r* | *b* | *b* | *a* | *b* | *a* | *c* |
| 1 | 0.45 | 0.41 | 0.22 | 0.21 | 0.61 | 0.58 | 0.84 | 0.17 |
| 2 | 0.70 | 0.45 | −1.00 | −0.83 | 0.82 | −0.51 | 0.91 | 0.17 |
| 3 | 0.65 | 0.50 | −0.75 | −0.60 | 0.92 | −0.28 | 1.10 | 0.17 |
| 4 | 0.77 | 0.20 | −1.45 | −2.25 | 0.34 | −1.69 | 0.37 | 0.17 |
| 5 | 0.75 | 0.37 | −1.34 | −1.25 | 0.66 | −0.97 | 0.69 | 0.17 |
| 6 | 0.39 | 0.27 | 0.52 | 0.71 | 0.39 | 1.11 | 0.64 | 0.17 |
| 7 | 0.76 | 0.40 | −1.36 | −1.67 | 0.75 | −0.90 | 0.79 | 0.17 |
| 8 | 0.60 | 0.35 | −0.52 | −0.56 | 0.52 | −0.09 | 0.67 | 0.17 |
| 9 | 0.78 | 0.29 | −1.51 | −1.70 | 0.50 | −1.36 | 0.53 | 0.17 |
| 10 | 0.55 | 0.32 | −0.27 | −0.32 | 0.47 | 0.19 | 0.62 | 0.17 |
| 11 | 0.61 | 0.37 | −0.53 | −0.55 | 0.56 | −0.14 | 0.65 | 0.17 |
| 12 | 0.59 | 0.21 | −0.47 | −0.81 | 0.29 | −0.11 | 0.37 | 0.17 |
| 13 | 0.55 | 0.30 | −0.25 | −0.30 | 0.43 | 0.22 | 0.56 | 0.17 |
| 14 | 0.73 | 0.44 | −1.18 | −0.97 | 0.82 | −0.67 | 0.88 | 0.17 |
| 15 | 0.38 | 0.54 | 0.58 | 0.49 | 0.75 | 0.76 | 1.30 | 0.15 |
| 16 | 0.62 | 0.54 | −0.58 | −0.45 | 1.04 | −0.04 | 1.53 | 0.21 |
| 17 | 0.80 | 0.34 | −1.67 | −1.53 | 0.67 | −1.32 | 0.66 | 0.17 |
| 18 | 0.65 | 0.45 | −0.74 | −0.78 | 0.55 | −0.32 | 0.66 | 0.17 |
| 19 | 0.49 | 0.43 | 0.04 | 0.03 | 0.68 | 0.51 | 1.23 | 0.22 |
| 20 | 0.64 | 0.40 | −0.70 | −0.66 | 0.65 | −0.31 | 0.73 | 0.17 |

**TABLE A.1** continued

| | | | | | | | | |
|---|---|---|---|---|---|---|---|---|
| | | | | *IRT Item Parameter Estimates* | | | | |
| | *Classical* | | *1P* | *2P* | | | *3P* | |
| *Item* | *p* | *r* | *b* | *b* | *a* | *b* | *a* | *c* |
| 21 | 0.69 | 0.34 | −0.99 | −1.07 | 0.53 | −0.68 | 0.59 | 0.17 |
| 22 | 0.67 | 0.41 | −0.85 | −0.78 | 0.68 | −0.46 | 0.74 | 0.10 |
| 23 | 0.46 | 0.35 | 0.18 | 0.20 | 0.50 | 0.63 | 0.74 | 0.17 |
| 24 | 0.74 | 0.52 | −1.26 | −0.89 | 1.15 | −0.64 | 1.25 | 0.17 |
| 25 | 0.61 | 0.47 | −0.56 | −0.48 | 0.80 | −0.12 | 0.98 | 0.17 |
| 26 | 0.34 | 0.30 | 0.78 | 0.97 | 0.44 | 1.18 | 0.65 | 0.12 |
| 27 | 0.70 | 0.50 | −1.05 | −0.80 | 0.99 | −0.52 | 1.08 | 0.17 |
| 28 | 0.61 | 0.44 | −0.56 | −0.50 | 0.73 | −0.12 | 0.91 | 0.17 |
| 29 | 0.73 | 0.35 | −1.23 | −1.24 | 0.58 | −0.91 | 0.62 | 0.17 |
| 30 | 0.74 | 0.44 | −1.28 | −1.03 | 0.85 | −0.81 | 0.86 | 0.17 |
| 31 | 0.57 | 0.32 | −0.35 | −0.41 | 0.46 | 0.08 | 0.58 | 0.17 |
| 32 | 0.74 | 0.38 | −1.26 | −1.17 | 0.65 | −0.90 | 0.68 | 0.17 |
| 33 | 0.44 | 0.35 | 0.29 | 0.32 | 0.52 | 0.78 | 0.87 | 0.19 |
| 34 | 0.60 | 0.45 | −0.52 | −0.46 | 0.75 | 0.03 | 1.10 | 0.20 |
| 35 | 0.28 | 0.29 | 1.14 | 1.37 | 0.46 | 1.40 | 1.04 | 0.15 |
| 36 | 0.69 | 0.46 | −0.99 | −0.82 | 0.83 | −0.50 | 0.94 | 0.17 |
| 37 | 0.29 | 0.27 | 1.11 | 1.46 | 0.41 | 1.54 | 0.63 | 0.10 |
| 38 | 0.77 | 0.35 | −1.43 | −1.39 | 0.62 | −1.10 | 0.64 | 0.17 |
| 39 | 0.60 | 0.38 | −0.50 | −0.51 | 0.57 | −0.09 | 0.69 | 0.17 |
| 40 | 0.43 | 0.48 | 0.33 | 0.26 | 0.81 | 0.58 | 1.50 | 0.17 |
| 41 | 0.43 | 0.41 | 0.33 | 0.3 | 0.62 | 0.68 | 0.99 | 0.17 |
| 42 | 0.60 | 0.46 | −0.51 | −0.45 | 0.75 | −0.09 | 0.93 | 0.17 |
| 43 | 0.46 | 0.37 | 0.17 | 0.18 | 0.56 | 0.76 | 1.23 | 0.25 |
| 44 | 0.52 | 0.23 | −0.12 | −0.19 | 0.32 | 0.44 | 0.41 | 0.17 |
| 45 | 0.26 | 0.28 | 1.24 | 1.53 | 0.45 | 1.46 | 1.14 | 0.15 |
| 46 | 0.64 | 0.44 | −0.68 | −0.61 | 0.73 | −0.25 | 0.84 | 0.17 |
| 47 | 0.75 | 0.40 | −1.34 | −1.16 | 0.74 | −0.89 | 0.78 | 0.17 |
| 48 | 0.79 | 0.39 | −1.57 | −1.30 | 0.79 | −1.08 | 0.80 | 0.17 |
| 49 | 0.76 | 0.36 | −1.37 | −1.28 | 0.65 | −1.00 | 0.68 | 0.17 |
| 50 | 0.57 | 0.30 | −0.34 | −0.43 | 0.41 | 0.10 | 0.51 | 0.17 |
| 51 | 0.49 | 0.35 | 0.04 | 0.05 | 0.53 | 0.57 | 0.94 | 0.20 |
| 52 | 0.34 | 0.37 | 0.81 | 0.81 | 0.59 | 1.01 | 1.06 | 0.14 |
| 53 | 0.50 | 0.39 | −0.04 | −0.41 | 0.59 | 0.53 | 1.01 | 0.23 |
| 54 | 0.74 | 0.33 | −1.26 | −1.32 | 0.55 | −0.94 | 0.61 | 0.17 |
| 55 | 0.48 | 0.61 | 0.12 | 0.05 | 1.21 | 0.22 | 1.43 | 0.08 |

**TABLE A.1** continued

| | *Classical* | | *1P* | *2P* | | *3P* | | |
|---|---|---|---|---|---|---|---|---|
| *Item* | *p* | *r* | *b* | *b* | *a* | *b* | *a* | *c* |
| 56 | 0.51 | 0.34 | −0.03 | −0.03 | 0.48 | 0.43 | 0.67 | 0.17 |
| 57 | 0.64 | 0.32 | −0.71 | −0.82 | 0.49 | −0.37 | 0.56 | 0.17 |
| 58 | 0.50 | 0.43 | −0.02 | −0.03 | 0.66 | 0.35 | 0.85 | 0.17 |
| 59 | 0.83 | 0.26 | −1.88 | −2.18 | 0.48 | −1.82 | 0.52 | 0.17 |
| 60 | 0.47 | 0.35 | 0.15 | 0.18 | 0.49 | 0.61 | 0.70 | 0.17 |
| 61 | 0.71 | 0.35 | −1.09 | −1.13 | 0.56 | −0.77 | 0.62 | 0.17 |
| 62 | 0.73 | 0.38 | −1.21 | −1.15 | 0.64 | −0.85 | 0.68 | 0.17 |
| 63 | 0.79 | 0.30 | −1.57 | −1.69 | 0.53 | −1.37 | 0.56 | 0.17 |
| 64 | 0.63 | 0.23 | −0.63 | −0.97 | 0.33 | −0.34 | 0.40 | 0.17 |
| 65 | 0.59 | 0.47 | −0.43 | −0.38 | 0.77 | −0.05 | 0.89 | 0.17 |
| 66 | 0.77 | 0.16 | −1.45 | −2.85 | 0.26 | −1.97 | 0.31 | 0.17 |
| 67 | 0.54 | 0.52 | −0.20 | −0.17 | 0.90 | 0.17 | 1.22 | 0.17 |
| 68 | 0.66 | 0.41 | −0.80 | −0.75 | 0.65 | −0.40 | 0.74 | 0.17 |
| 69 | 0.72 | 0.37 | −1.12 | −1.10 | 0.61 | −0.77 | 0.66 | 0.17 |
| 70 | 0.53 | 0.21 | −0.14 | −0.26 | 0.26 | 0.46 | 0.35 | 0.17 |
| 71 | 0.78 | 0.41 | −1.49 | −1.21 | 0.83 | −0.98 | 0.84 | 0.17 |
| 72 | 0.78 | 0.37 | −1.53 | −1.34 | 0.72 | −1.06 | 0.76 | 0.17 |
| 73 | 0.64 | 0.53 | −0.68 | −0.53 | 0.98 | −0.23 | 1.14 | 0.17 |
| 74 | 0.60 | 0.28 | −0.48 | −0.62 | 0.41 | −0.07 | 0.52 | 0.17 |
| 75 | 0.46 | 0.23 | 0.17 | 0.31 | 0.30 | 0.91 | 1.41 | 0.17 |
| 76 | | | 1.26 | | | | | |
| 77 | | | −1.47 | | | | | |
| 78 | | | −1.61 | | | | | |
| 79 | | | 0.60 | | | | | |
| 80 | | | 0.63 | | | | | |
| 81 | | | −1.45 | | | | | |
| 82 | | | −0.91 | | | | | |
| 83 | | | −0.69 | | | | | |
| 84 | | | 1.15 | | | | | |
| 85 | | | 1.02 | | | | | |
| 86 | | | 0.91 | | | | | |
| 87 | | | −0.39 | | | | | |
| 88 | | | 2.11 | | | | | |
| 89 | | | 1.78 | | | | | |
| 90 | | | 1.96 | | | | | |

# Appendix B

## Sources for IRT Computer Programs

| *Program* | *Source* |
|---|---|
| BICAL,<br>BIGSCALE | Dr. Benjamin Wright<br>University of Chicago<br>Statistical Laboratory<br>Department of Education<br>5835 Kimbark Ave.<br>Chicago, IL 60637<br>U.S.A. |
| MICROSCALE | Mediax Interactive Technologies<br>21 Charles Street<br>Westport, CT 06880<br>U.S.A. |
| PML | Dr. Jan-Eric Gustafsson<br>University of Göteborg<br>Institute of Education<br>Fack S-431 20<br>Molndal<br>SWEDEN |
| RASCAL,<br>ASCAL | Assessment Systems Corporation<br>2233 University Avenue<br>Suite 440<br>St. Paul, MN 55114<br>U.S.A. |
| RIDA | Dr. Cees Glas<br>National Institute for Educational Measurement<br>P.O. Box 1034<br>6801 MG Arnhem<br>The Netherlands |

| *Program* | *Source* |
|-----------|----------|
| LOGIST | Educational Testing Service<br>Rosedale Road<br>Princeton, NJ 08541<br>U.S.A. |
| BILOG,<br>MULTILOG | Scientific Software, Inc.<br>1369 Neitzel Road<br>Mooresville, IN 46158<br>U.S.A. |
| NOHARM | Dr. Colin Fraser<br>Centre for Behavioral Studies<br>University of New England<br>Armidale, N.S.W.<br>AUSTRALIA 2351 |
| MIRTE | Dr. Mark Reckase<br>American College Testing Program<br>P.O. Box 168<br>Iowa City, IA 52243<br>U.S.A. |

# References

American Educational Research Association, American Psychological Association, & National Council on Measurement in Education (1985). *Standards for educational and psychological testing.* Washington, DC: American Psychological Association.

Andersen, E. B. (1972). The numerical solution of a set of conditional estimation equations. *Journal of the Royal Statistical Society, Series B, 34,* 42-54.

Andersen, E. B. (1973). A goodness of fit test for the Rasch model. *Psychometrika, 38,* 123-140.

Andrich, D. (1978a). Application of a psychometric rating model to ordered categories which are scored with successive integers. *Applied Psychological Measurement, 2,* 581-594.

Andrich, D. (1978b). A binomial latent trait model for the study of Likert-style attitude questionnaires. *British Journal of Mathematical and Statistical Psychology, 31,* 84-98.

Andrich, D. (1978c). A rating formulation for ordered response categories. *Psychometrika, 43,* 561-573.

Andrich, D. (1982). An extension of the Rasch model for ratings providing both location and dispersion parameters. *Psychometrika, 47,* 105-113.

Angoff, W. H. (1971). Scales, norms, and equivalent scores. In R. L. Thorndike (Ed.), *Educational measurement* (2nd ed.) (pp. 508-600). Washington, DC: American Council on Education.

Ansley, T. N., & Forsyth, R. A. (1985). An examination of the characteristics of unidimensional IRT parameter estimates derived from two-dimensional data. *Applied Psychological Measurement, 9*(1), 37-48.

Assessment Systems Corporation. (1988). *User's manual for the MicroCAT testing system.* (Version 3). St. Paul, MN: Author.

Baker, F. B. (1964). An intersection of test score interpretation and item analysis. *Journal of Educational Measurement, 1,* 23-28.

Baker, F. B. (1965). Origins of the item parameters $X_{50}$ and $\beta$ as a modern item analysis technique. *Journal of Educational Measurement, 2,* 167-180.

Baker, F. B. (1985). *The basics of item response theory.* Portsmouth, NH: Heinemann.

Baker, F. B. (1987). Methodology review: Item parameter estimation under the one-, two-, and three-parameter logistic models. *Applied Psychological Measurement, 11,* 111-142.

161

Bejar, I. I. (1980). A procedure for investigating the unidimensionality of achievement tests based on item parameter estimates. *Journal of Educational Measurement, 17,* 283-296.

Birnbaum, A. (1968). Some latent trait models and their use in inferring an examinee's ability. In F. M. Lord and M. R. Novick, *Statistical theories of mental test scores* (chapters 17-20). Reading, MA: Addison-Wesley.

Bock, R. D. (1972). Estimating item parameters and latent ability when responses are scored in two or more nominal categories. *Psychometrika, 37,* 29-51.

Bock, R. D., & Aitkin, M. (1981). Marginal maximum likelihood estimation of item parameters: Application of an EM algorithm. *Psychometrika, 46,* 443-459.

Bock, R. D., Gibbons, R., & Muraki, E. (1988). Full information item factor analysis. *Applied Psychological Measurement, 12*(3), 261-280.

Bock, R. D., & Lieberman, M. (1970). Fitting a response curve model for dichotomously scored items. *Psychometrika, 35,* 179-198.

Bock, R. D., & Mislevy, R. J. (1982). Adaptive EAP estimation of ability in a microcomputer environment. *Applied Psychological Measurement, 6*(4), 431-444.

Bunderson, C. V., Inouye, D. K., & Olsen, J. B. (1989). The four generations of computerized educational measurement. In R. L. Linn (Ed.), *Educational measurement* (3rd ed.) (pp. 367-407). New York: Macmillan.

Carlson, J. E. (1987). *Multidimensional item response theory estimation: A computer program* (Research Report ONR87-2). Iowa City, IA: American College Testing.

Cook, L. L., & Eignor, D. R. (1983). Practical considerations regarding the use of item response theory to equate tests. In R. K. Hambleton (Ed.), *Applications of item response theory* (pp. 175-195). Vancouver, BC: Educational Research Institute of British Columbia.

Cook, L. L., & Eignor, D. R. (1989). Using item response theory in test score equating. *International Journal of Educational Research, 13*(2), 161-173.

Cook, L. L., Eignor, D. R., & Taft, H. L. (1988). A comparative study of the effects of recency of instruction on the stability of IRT and conventional item parameter estimates. *Journal of Educational Measurement, 25*(1), 31-45.

de Gruijter, D. N. M. (1986). Small *N* does not always justify the Rasch model. *Applied Psychological Measurement, 10,* 187-194.

de Gruijter, D. N. M., & Hambleton, R. K. (1983). Using item response models in criterion-referenced test item selection. In R. K. Hambleton (Ed.), *Applications of item response theory* (pp. 142-154). Vancouver, BC: Educational Research Institute of British Columbia.

Divgi, D. R. (1986). Does the Rasch model really work for multiple choice items? Not if you look closely. *Journal of Educational Measurement, 23,* 283-298.

Drasgow, F., Levine, M. V., & McLaughlin, M. E. (1987). Detecting inappropriate test scores with optimal and practical appropriateness indices. *Applied Psychological Measurement, 11*(1), 59-79.

Drasgow, F., & Lissak, R. I. (1983). Modified parallel analysis: A procedure for examining the latent dimensionality of dichotomously scored item responses. *Journal of Applied Psychology, 68,* 363-373.

Drasgow, F., & Parsons, C. K. (1983). Application of unidimensional item response theory models to multidimensional data. *Applied Psychological Measurement, 7,* 189-199.

Embretson, S. E. (1984). A general latent trait model for response processes. *Psychometrika, 49,* 175-186.

Fraser, C., & McDonald, R. P. (1988). NOHARM: Least squares item factor analysis. *Multivariate Behavioral Research, 23,* 267-269.

Glas, C. (1990). *RIDA: Rasch incomplete design analysis.* Arnhem, The Netherlands: National Institute for Educational Measurement.

Goldstein, H., & Wood, R. (1989). Five decades of item response modelling. *British Journal of Mathematical and Statistical Psychology, 42,* 139-167.

Green, B. F., Bock, R. D., Humphreys, L. G., Linn, R. L., & Reckase, M. D. (1984). Technical guidelines for assessing computerized adaptive tests. *Journal of Educational Measurement, 21*(4), 347-360.

Green, D. R., Yen, W. M., & Burket, G. R. (1989). Experiences in the application of item response theory in test construction. *Applied Measurement in Education, 2*(4), 297-312.

Gulliksen, H. (1950). *Theory of mental tests.* New York: John Wiley.

Gustafsson, J. E. (1980a). A solution of the conditional estimation problem for long tests in the Rasch model for dichotomous items. *Educational and Psychological Measurement, 40,* 377-385.

Gustafsson, J. E. (1980b). Testing and obtaining fit of data to the Rasch model. *British Journal of Mathematical and Statistical Psychology, 33,* 205-233.

Haebara, T. (1980). Equating logistic ability scales by weighted least squares method. *Japanese Psychological Research, 22,* 144-149.

Hambleton, R. K. (Ed.). (1983). *Applications of item response theory.* Vancouver, BC: Educational Research Institute of British Columbia.

Hambleton, R. K. (1989). Principles and selected applications of item response theory. In R. L. Linn (Ed.), *Educational measurement* (3rd ed.) (pp. 147-200). New York: Macmillan.

Hambleton, R. K., & Cook, L. L. (1983). Robustness of item response models and effects of test length and sample size on the precision of ability estimates. In D. Weiss (Ed.), *New horizons in testing* (pp. 31-49). New York: Academic Press.

Hambleton, R. K., & de Gruijter, D. N. M. (1983). Application of item response models to criterion-referenced test item selection. *Journal of Educational Measurement, 20,* 355-367.

Hambleton, R. K., Jones, R. W., & Rogers, H. J. (1990, August). *Influence of item parameter estimation errors in test development.* Paper presented at the meeting of American Psychological Association, Boston.

Hambleton, R. K., & Rogers, H. J. (1989). Detecting potentially biased test items: Comparison of IRT area and Mantel-Haenszel methods. *Applied Measurement in Education, 2*(4), 313-334.

Hambleton, R. K., & Rogers, H. J. (in press). Assessment of IRT model fit. *Applied Psychological Measurement.*

Hambleton, R. K., & Rovinelli, R. J. (1973). A Fortran IV program for generating examinee response data from logistic test models. *Behavioral Science, 17,* 73-74.

Hambleton, R. K., & Rovinelli, R. J. (1986). Assessing the dimensionality of a set of test items. *Applied Psychological Measurement, 10,* 287-302.

Hambleton, R. K., & Swaminathan, H. (1985). *Item response theory: Principles and applications.* Boston: Kluwer.

Hambleton, R. K., & Traub, R. E. (1973). Analysis of empirical data using two logistic latent trait models. *British Journal of Mathematical and Statistical Psychology, 26,* 273-281.

Hambleton, R. K., & van der Linden, W. J. (1982). Advances in item response theory and applications: An introduction. *Applied Psychological Measurement, 6,* 373-378.

Hambleton, R. K., Zaal, J. N., & Pieters, J. M. P. (1991). Computerized adaptive testing: Theory, applications, and standards. In R. K. Hambleton & J. N. Zaal (Eds.), *Advances in educational and psychological testing: Theory and applications* (pp. 341-366). Boston: Kluwer.

Harris, D. (1989). Comparison of 1-, 2-, and 3-parameter IRT models. *Educational Measurement: Issues and Practice, 8,* 35-41.

Hattie, J. A. (1985). Methodological review: Assessing unidimensionality of tests and items. *Applied Psychological Measurement, 9,* 139-164.

Holland, P. W., & Thayer, D. T. (1988). Differential item performance and the Mantel-Haenszel procedure. In H. Wainer & H. I. Braun (Eds.), *Test validity* (pp. 129-145). Hillsdale, NJ: Lawrence Erlbaum.

Horn, J. L. (1965). A rationale and test for the number of factors in factor analysis. *Psychometrika, 30,* 179-185.

Kendall, M. G., & Stuart, A. (1961). *The advanced theory of statistics* (Vol. I). New York: Hafner.

Kingsbury, G. G., & Zara, A. R. (1989). Procedures for selecting items for computerized adaptive tests. *Applied Measurement in Education, 2*(4), 359-375.

Kingston, N. M., & Dorans, N. J. (1984). Item location effects and their implications for IRT equating and adaptive testing. *Applied Psychological Measurement, 8,* 147-154.

Kingston, N. M., & Dorans, N. J. (1985). The analysis of item-ability regressions: An exploratory IRT model fit tool. *Applied Psychological Measurement, 9,* 281-288.

Kingston, N. M., & Stocking, M. (1986, August). *Psychometric issues in IRT-based test construction.* Paper presented at the meeting of American Psychological Association, Washington, DC.

Klein, L. W., & Jarjoura, D. (1985). The importance of content representation for common-item equating with non-random groups. *Journal of Educational Measurement, 22*(3), 197-206.

Kolen, M. J. (1988). Traditional equating methodology. *Educational Measurement: Issues and Practice, 7*(4), 29-36.

Linn, R. L. (1990). Has item response theory increased the validity of achievement test scores? *Applied Measurement in Education, 3*(2), 115-141.

Linn, R. L., & Hambleton, R. K. (1990). *Customized tests and customized norms* (CRESST Technical Report). Los Angeles: UCLA, School of Education.

Linn, R. L., & Harnisch, D. L. (1981). Interactions between item content and group membership on achievement test items. *Journal of Educational Measurement, 18,* 109-118.

Linn, R. L., Levine, M. V., Hastings, C. N., & Wardrop, J. L. (1981). Item bias in a test of reading comprehension. *Applied Psychological Measurement, 5,* 159-173.

Lord, F. M. (1952). *A theory of test scores* (Psychometric Monograph No. 7). Iowa City, IA: Psychometric Society.

Lord, F. M. (1974). Estimation of latent ability and item parameters when there are omitted responses. *Psychometrika, 39,* 247-264.

Lord, F. M. (1977). Practical applications of item characteristic curve theory. *Journal of Educational Measurement, 14,* 117-138.

Lord, F. M. (1980). *Applications of item response theory to practical testing problems.* Hillsdale, NJ: Lawrence Erlbaum.

Lord, F. M. (1984). Standard errors of measurement at different ability levels. *Journal of Educational Measurement, 21,* 239-243.

Lord, F. M., & Novick, M. R. (1968). *Statistical theories of mental test scores.* Reading, MA: Addison-Wesley.

Ludlow, L. H. (1985). A strategy for the graphical representation of Rasch model residuals. *Educational and Psychological Measurement, 45,* 851-859.

Ludlow, L. H. (1986). Graphical analysis of item response theory residuals. *Applied Psychological Measurement, 10,* 217-229.

Masters, G. N. (1982). A Rasch model for partial credit scoring. *Psychometrika, 47,* 149-174.

Masters, G. N., & Wright, B. D. (1984). The essential process in a family of measurement models. *Psychometrika, 49,* 529-544.

McDonald, R. P. (1967). *Non-linear factor analysis* (Psychometric Monograph No. 15). Iowa City: IA: Psychometric Society.

McDonald, R. P. (1981). The dimensionality of tests and items. *British Journal of Mathematical and Statistical Psychology, 34,* 100-117.

McDonald, R. P. (1989). Future directions for item response theory. *International Journal of Educational Research, 13*(2), 205-220.

McLaughlin, M. E., & Drasgow, F. (1987). Lord's chi-square test of item bias with estimated and with known person parameters. *Applied Psychological Measurement, 11,* 161-173.

Mediax Interactive Technologies. (1986). *Microscale.* Black Rock, CT: Author.

Mellenbergh, G. (1989). Item bias and item response theory. *International Journal of Educational Research, 13*(2), 127-143.

Millman, J., & Arter, J. A. (1984). Issues in item banking. *Journal of Educational Measurement, 21,* 315-330.

Mislevy, R. J. (1986). Bayes modal estimation in item response models. *Psychometrika, 51,* 177-195.

Mislevy, R. J., & Bock, R. D. (1984). *BILOG: Maximum likelihood item analysis and test scoring with logistic models.* Mooresville, IN: Scientific Software.

Owen, R. J. (1975). A Bayesian sequential procedure for quantal response in the context of adaptive mental testing. *Journal of the American Statistical Association, 70,* 351-356.

Phillips, S. E., & Mehrens, W. A. (1987). Curricular differences and unidimensionality of achievement test data: An exploratory analysis. *Journal of Educational Measurement, 24,* 1-16.

Raju, N. S. (1988). The area between two item characteristic curves. *Psychometrika, 53,* 495-502.

Raju, N. S. (1990). Determining the significance of estimated signed and unsigned areas between two item response functions. *Applied Psychological Measurement, 14*(2), 197-207.

Rasch, G. (1960). *Probabilistic models for some intelligence and attainment tests.* Copenhagen: Danish Institute for Educational Research.

Reckase, M. D. (1979). Unifactor latent trait models applied to multi-factor tests: Results and implications. *Journal of Educational Statistics, 4,* 207-230.

Reshetar, R. (1990). *Computer adaptive testing: Development and application* (Laboratory of Psychometric and Evaluative Research Report No. 204). Amherst: University of Massachusetts, School of Education.

Rogers, H. J., & Hambleton, R. K. (1989). Evaluation of computer simulated baseline statistics for use in item bias studies. *Educational and Psychological Measurement, 49*, 355-369.

Rogers, H. J., & Hattie, J. A. (1987). A Monte Carlo investigation of several person and item fit statistics for item response models. *Applied Psychological Measurement, 11*, 47-57.

Rudner, L. M., Getson, P. R., & Knight, D. L. (1980). Biased item detection techniques. *Journal of Educational Statistics, 5*, 213-233.

Safrit, M. J., Costa, M. G., & Cohen, A. S. (1989). Item response theory and the measurement of motor behavior. *Research Quarterly for Exercise and Sport, 60*, 325-335.

Samejima, F. (1969). *Estimation of latent ability using a response pattern of graded scores* (Psychometric Monograph No. 17). Iowa City, IA: Psychometric Society.

Samejima, F. (1972). *A general model for free response data* (Psychometric Monograph No. 18). Iowa City, IA: Psychometric Society.

Samejima, F. (1973). Homogeneous case of the continuous response model. *Psychometrika, 38*, 203-219.

Samejima, F. (1974). Normal ogive model on the continuous response level in the multidimensional latent space. *Psychometrika, 39*, 111-121.

Samejima, F. (1977). A use of the information function in tailored testing. *Applied Psychological Measurement, 1*, 233-247.

Shepard, L. A., Camilli, G., & Averill, M. (1981). Comparison of procedures for detecting test-item bias with both internal and external ability criteria. *Journal of Educational Statistics, 6*, 317-375.

Shepard, L. A., Camilli, G., & Williams, D. M. (1984). Accounting for statistical artifacts in item bias research. *Journal of Educational Statistics, 9*, 93-128.

Shepard, L. A., Camilli, G., & Williams, D. M. (1985). Validity of approximation techniques for detecting item bias. *Journal of Educational Measurement, 22*(2), 77-105.

Spray, J. (1990). One-parameter item response theory models for psychomotor tests involving repeated, independent attempts. *Research Quarterly for Exercise and Sport, 61*(2), 162-168.

Stocking, M. L. (1990). Specifying optimum examinees for item parameter estimation in item response theory. *Psychometrika, 55*(3), 461-475.

Stocking, M. L., & Lord, F. M. (1983). Developing a common metric in item response theory. *Applied Psychological Measurement, 7*, 201-210.

Subkoviak, M. J., Mack, J. S., Ironson, G. H., & Craig, R. D. (1984). Empirical comparison of selected item bias detection procedures with bias manipulation. *Journal of Educational Measurement, 21*(1), 49-58.

Swaminathan, H. (1983). Parameter estimation in item-response models. In R. K. Hambleton (Ed.), *Applications of item response theory* (pp. 24-44). Vancouver, BC: Educational Research Institute of British Columbia.

Swaminathan, H., & Gifford, J. A. (1982). Bayesian estimation in the Rasch model. *Journal of Educational Statistics, 7*, 175-191.

Swaminathan, H., & Gifford, J. A. (1983). Estimation of parameters in the three-parameter latent trait model. In D. Weiss (Ed.), *New horizons in testing* (pp. 13-30). New York: Academic Press.

Swaminathan, H., & Gifford, J. A. (1985). Bayesian estimation in the two-parameter logistic model. *Psychometrika, 50,* 349-364.

Swaminathan, H., & Gifford, J. A. (1986). Bayesian estimation in the three-parameter logistic model. *Psychometrika, 51,* 589-601.

Swaminathan, H., & Rogers, H. J. (1990). Detecting differential item functioning using logistic regression procedures. *Journal of Educational Measurement, 27*(4), 361-370.

Tatsuoka, K. K. (1987). Validation of cognitive sensitivity for item response curves. *Journal of Educational Measurement, 24,* 233-245.

Thissen, D. M. (1986). *MULTILOG: Item analysis and scoring with multiple category response models* (Version 5). Mooresville, IN: Scientific Software.

Thissen, D. M., & Steinberg, L. (1986). A taxonomy of item response models. *Psychometrika, 51,* 567-577.

Traub, R. E., & Lam, R. (1985). Latent structure and item sampling models for testing. *Annual Review of Psychology, 36,* 19-48.

Traub, R. E., & Wolfe, R. G. (1981). Latent trait theories and the assessment of educational achievement. In D. C. Berliner (Ed.), *Review of research in education* (pp. 377-435). Washington, DC: American Educational Research Association.

Tucker, L. R., Humphreys, L. G., & Roznowski, M. A. (1986). *Comparative accuracy of five indices of dimensionality of binary items.* Champaign-Urbana: University of Illinois, Department of Psychology.

Urry, V. W. (1974). Approximations to item parameters of mental test models and their uses. *Educational and Psychological Measurement, 34,* 253-269.

Urry, V. W. (1978). *ANCILLES: Item parameter estimation program with normal ogive and logistic three-parameter model options.* Washington, DC: U.S. Civil Service Commission, Development Center.

Vale, C. D. (1986). Linking item parameters onto a common scale. *Applied Psychological Measurement, 10*(4), 333-344.

van der Linden, W. J., & Boekkooi-Timminga, E. (1989). A maximum model for test design with practical constraints. *Psychometrika, 54*(2), 237-247.

Wainer, H. et al. (Eds.). (1990). *Computerized adaptive testing: A primer.* Hillsdale, NJ: Lawrence Erlbaum.

Wainer, H., & Thissen, D. (1987). Estimating ability with the wrong model. *Journal of Educational Statistics, 12,* 339-368.

Weiss, D. J. (1982). Improving measurement quality and efficiency with adaptive testing. *Applied Psychological Measurement, 6,* 473-492.

Weiss, D. J. (Ed.). (1983). *New horizons in testing.* New York: Academic Press.

Weiss, D. J. (1985). Adaptive testing by computer. *Journal of Consulting and Clinical Psychology, 53,* 774-789.

Weiss, D. J., & Kingsbury, G. G. (1984). Application of computerized adaptive testing to educational problems. *Journal of Educational Measurement, 21,* 361-375.

Wingersky, M. S. (1983). LOGIST: A program for computing maximum likelihood procedures for logistic test models. In R. K. Hambleton (Ed.), *Applications of item response theory* (pp. 45-56). Vancouver, BC: Educational Research Institute of British Columbia.

Wingersky, M. S., Barton, M. A., & Lord, F. M. (1982). *LOGIST user's guide*. Princeton, NJ: Educational Testing Service.

Woodcock, R. W. (1978). *Development and standardization of the Woodcock-Johnson Psycho-Educational Battery*. Hingham, MA: Teaching Resources Corporation.

Wright, B. D. (1968). Sample-free test calibration and person measurement. *Proceedings of the 1967 Invitational Conference on Testing Problems*. Princeton, NJ: Educational Testing Service.

Wright, B. D. (1977). Solving measurement problems with the Rasch model. *Journal of Educational Measurement, 14,* 97-116.

Wright, B. D., Mead, R. J., & Bell, S. R. (1979). *BICAL: Calibrating items with the Rasch model* (Statistical Laboratory Research Memorandum No. 23B). Chicago: University of Chicago, School of Education.

Wright, B. D., Schulz, M., & Linacre, J. M. (1989). *BIGSCALE: Rasch analysis computer program*. Chicago: MESA Press.

Wright, B. D., & Stone, M. H. (1979). *Best test design*. Chicago: MESA Press.

Yen, W. M. (1980). The extent, causes, and importance of context effects on item parameters for two latent trait models. *Journal of Educational Measurement, 17,* 297-311.

Yen, W. M. (1981). Using simulation results to choose a latent trait model. *Applied Psychological Measurement, 5,* 245-262.

Yen, M. W. (1983). Use of the three-parameter logistic model in the development of a standardized achievement test. In R. K. Hambleton (Ed.), *Applications of item response theory* (pp. 123-141). Vancouver, BC: Educational Research Institute of British Columbia.

Yen, W. M., Burket, G. R., & Sykes, R. C. (in press). Non-unique solutions to the likelihood equation for the three-parameter logistic model. *Psychometrika*.

# Index

# About the Authors

**Ronald K. Hambleton** is Professor of Education and Psychology and Chairman of the Laboratory of Psychometric and Evaluative Research at the University of Massachusetts at Amherst. He received his Ph.D. in psychometric methods from the University of Toronto in 1969. His principal research interests are in the areas of criterion-referenced measurement and item response theory. His most recent books are *Item Response Theory: Principles and Applications* (co-authored with H. Swaminathan), *A Practical Guide to Criterion-Referenced Testing,* and, forthcoming, *Advances in Educational and Psychological Testing* (co-edited with Jac Zaal). He has served as an Associate Editor to the *Journal of Educational Statistics* (1981-1989) and currently serves on the editorial boards of *Applied Measurement in Education, Multivariate Behavioral Research, Applied Psychological Measurement, Journal of Educational Measurement, Educational and Psychological Measurement, Evaluation and the Health Professions,* and *Psicothema.* He has served also as President of the International Test Commission (1990-1994) and as President of the National Council on Measurement in Education (1989-1990).

**H. Swaminathan** is Professor of Education and Psychology at the University of Massachusetts at Amherst. He received his Ph.D. in psychometric methods and statistics from the University of Toronto in 1971. He has held the positions of Associate Dean of Academic Affairs and Acting Dean of the School of Education. He has served as an Associate Editor to the *Journal of Educational Statistics* and currently is an Associate Editor of *Psicothema* and *Revista Educao Potuguese.* He has served also as the President of Educational Statisticians, a special interest group of the American Educational Research Association; co-program chair of Division D of AERA; and as a member of the

Graduate Records Examinations Board. His principal research interests are in the areas of item response theory, multivariate statistics, and Bayesian analysis.

**H. Jane Rogers** is Assistant Professor at Teachers College, Columbia University. She received her Ph.D. in psychometric methods from the University of Massachusetts in 1989. Her research interests include item response theory, large-scale assessment, methods for the detection of differential item functioning, Bayesian methods, and multivariate statistics.